CLASSICS

EDMONDS®
CLASSICS

hachette
NEW ZEALAND

ISBN: 978-1-86971-033-0

Published in 2005 by Hachette Livre New Zealand Ltd

Reprinted 2006 (twice), 2007, 2009, 2010 (twice), 2011, 2012

This edition published in 2015 by Hachette New Zealand Ltd.
Level 2, 23 O'Connell Street, Auckland, New Zealand

Cover and text design by Seymour Designs
Typeset by Bookhouse, Sydney
Printed by 1010 Printing, China

CONTENTS

Thomas Edmonds (Canterbury Museum)

THE STORY OF EDMONDS

Twenty-year-old Thomas John Edmonds arrived in Lyttelton in 1879. He set up business as a grocer on the corner of Randolph and Edmonds Streets. Thomas soon saw there was a need for reliable good quality baking powder, and began mixing his own concoction in a small room behind the shop using his past experience working for a confectioner in London.

A small batch of 200 tins of trial baking powder found a ready sale among Thomas Edmonds' customers and a small but consistent demand developed. Encouraged by this, he spent three years improving his product while other brands appeared on the market.

One day, a doubting customer asked if this baking powder was any good. The grocer replied, 'It is sure to rise, Madam.' Struck with the aptness of his own remarks, he used it to design the famous trademark with the rising sun.

Prompted by his customers' testimonials, Mr Edmonds placed the perfected baking powder on the market, and then waited for the demand to develop. Three months later there had been no orders from the merchants who had placed samples of 'Sure to Rise' on their shelves; the public did not know the brand.

Mr Edmonds began to canvass the local Canterbury region. His practice was to leave a tin of baking powder with almost every householder, whether they wished to buy it or not, agreeing to take it back on his next visit if they were not satisfied. Apparently, no tins were returned.

Soon, orders for Edmonds Baking Powder increased. In 1889, Mr Edmonds won two first prizes for his baking powder and egg powder at the Dunedin Exhibition. At the New Zealand International Exhibition cooking competition in 1906, five first prizes included Edmonds Baking Powder. Around the turn of the century, Mr Edmonds moved to a house in Ferry Road and built sheds behind it to allow him to make baking powder on a larger scale. He also started making custard powder. By 1928, sales of Edmonds Baking Powder had hit 2.5 million.

The first *Edmonds Cookery Book* appeared in 1908. Couples throughout New Zealand could apply to receive a free copy of the cookbook on their engagement. Mr Edmonds retired in 1911, although he still maintained an active interest in the business until his death in 1932. The factory that has appeared on the *Edmonds Cookery Book* since 1955 was built in 1922, when the award-winning gardens were also established.

The *Edmonds Cookery Book* has become the biggest selling book ever published in New Zealand. It is estimated that over 4 million copies of the book have been sold since the first edition in 1908.

WHAT IS YOUR FAVOURITE EDMONDS RECIPE?

In November 2014, we asked New Zealanders (through a competition in the *New Zealand Woman's Weekly*) this question. People didn't just reply with a recipe, they told us why. The *Edmonds Cookery Book* is the stuff of memories. The scents are ingrained in our childhoods, the flavours remind us of people we love and the results earn us kudos in our social circle. The cookbook is almost like a family's favourite aunt – thoroughly reliable, always helpful and regarded with great affection . . .

But, of course, the recipes were the stars and there were many favourites. All these have been collected in *Edmonds Classics: New Zealand's Favourite Recipes* and we have marked the top-ranked recipes with 'Edmonds Top 20'. The winners were (in order of votes received):

1. Banana Cake
2. Afghans
3. Ginger Crunch
4. Scones
5. Pikelets
6. Santé / Chocolate Chip Biscuits
7. Mustard Sauce
8. Anzac Biscuits
9. Peanut Brownies
10. Shortbread
11. One-Egg Chocolate Cake
12. Yoyos
13. Cheese Scones
14. Pavlova
15. Louise Cake
16. Bacon & Egg Pie
17. Cinnamon Cream Oysters
18. Hokey Pokey Biscuits
19. Cup Cakes
20. Carrot Cake

Many of you will be glad to find old favourites, long since removed from the *Edmonds Cookery Book*, reappearing here. Now cooks can once again enjoy Marshmallow Shortcake, Coconut Crispettes, Louise Cake, Mock Whitebait Patties, Beef Stew, Carrot Plum Pudding and many more of the old classics. We hope that these recipes will inspire a new generation of New Zealand cooks to continue making the recipes that so delighted past generations.

WHY RECIPES CHANGE

We often get asked why recipes have been removed from the *Edmonds Cookery Book* and why recipe ingredients or quantities change. New Zealand's population is constantly changing as are world trends in food and diet. The recipes selected for the *Edmonds Cookery Book* reflect the 'face of New Zealand': recipes that the modern or average New Zealander would want to and be able to cook. In order to add new recipes, some old ones need to be removed. Otherwise we would have a very large and very expensive cookbook!

Often a recipe is retested and adapted when ingredients are no longer readily available. For example, the recipe for Coffee Cake was rewritten when chicory essence became difficult to come by and angelica was left out of Tennis Biscuits as it is now hard for the home cook to obtain.

Over time, quantities sometimes change for processed products. The weight of the flour we use today is different from the flour used by previous generations as it is more finely processed. Likewise, the strength of spices such as cayenne pepper or mustard has increased so the quantity in recipes has been reduced. And, of course, cooking times and temperatures were reduced when thermostatically controlled ovens were introduced.

We always try to adapt Edmonds recipes to be current and accurate, so that your cakes are still 'sure to rise' and every dish is delicious.

Note: Older editions of the *Edmonds Cookery Book* did not give information on the number of servings a recipe made. This information was introduced in the 1980s. Therefore older recipes appearing in *Edmonds Classics* do not include serving information.

WEIGHTS AND MEASURES

- New Zealand Standard metric cup and spoon measures are used in all recipes.

- All measurements are level.

- Easy measuring — use measuring cups or jugs for liquid measures and sets of 1 cup, ½ cup, ⅓ cup and ¼ cup for dry ingredients.

- Brown sugar measurements — are firmly packed so that the sugar will hold the shape of the cup when tipped out.

- Eggs — No. 6 eggs are used as the standard size.

ABBREVIATIONS

l	= litre
ml	= millilitre
cm	= centimetre
mm	= millimetre
g	= gram
kg	= kilogram
°C	= degrees celsius

STANDARD MEASURES ARE

1 cup	=	250 millilitres
1 litre	=	4 cups
1 tablespoon	=	15 millilitres
1 dessertspoon	=	10 millilitres
1 teaspoon	=	5 millilitres
½ teaspoon	=	2.5 millilitres
¼ teaspoon	=	1.25 millilitres

APPROXIMATE METRIC/ IMPERIAL CONVERSIONS IN COMMON COOKING USE

WEIGHT

25 g	=	1 ounce
125 g	=	4 ounces
225 g	=	8 ounces
500 g	=	1 pound

VOLUME

1 kg	=	2¼ pounds
1 litre	=	1¾ pints

MEASUREMENTS

1 cm	=	½ inch
20 cm	=	8 inches
30 cm	=	12 inches

APPROXIMATE EQUIVALENTS

ITEM	MEASURE	EQUIVALENT
breadcrumbs (fresh)	1 cup	50 g
butter	2 tablespoons	30 g
cheese (grated, firmly packed)	1 cup	100 g
cocoa	4 tablespoons	25 g
coconut	1 cup	75 g
cornflour	4 tablespoons	25 g
cream	½ pint	300 ml
dried fruit (currants, sultanas, raisins, dates)	1 cup	150–175 g
flour	1 cup	125 g
gelatine	4 tablespoons	25 g
golden syrup	1 tablespoon	25 g
milk	1 cup	250 ml
nuts	1 cup	125–150 g
oil	1 tablespoon	15 ml
	2 tablespoons	25 g
rice, sago	1 cup	200 g
salt	2 tablespoons	25 g
sour cream	1 cup	250 g
sugar, white	2 tablespoons	30 g
	1 cup	250 g
sugar, brown	1 cup (firmly packed)	200 g
	(loosely packed)	125–150 g
icing	1 cup	150 g
standard No.6 egg		50 g (approx.)

BEFORE AND AFTER EQUIVALENT MEASURES —
APPROXIMATE AMOUNTS NEEDED TO GIVE MEASURES

$^1/_3$ cup uncooked rice = 1 cup cooked rice
$^1/_3$ cup uncooked pasta = 1 cup cooked pasta
2–3 chicken pieces = 1 cup cooked chicken
100 g cheese = 1 cup grated cheese
75 g mushrooms = 1 cup sliced = ½ cup cooked
4 toast slices bread = 1 cup fresh breadcrumbs
200 g (two) potatoes = 1 cup mashed potato

OVEN TEMPERATURE CONVERSIONS

160°C = 325°F   190°C = 375°F
180°C = 350°F   200°C = 400°F

A GUIDE TO OVEN TEMPERATURES AND USE

PRODUCT	°C	°F	GAS No.	DESCRIPTION
meringues, pavlova	110–140	225–275	¼–1	slow
custards, milk puddings, shortbread, rich fruit cakes, casseroles, slow roasting	150–160	300–325	2–3	moderately slow
biscuits, large and small cakes	180–190	350–375	4–5	moderate
roasting, sponges, muffins, short pastry	190–220	375–425	5–6	moderately hot
flaky pastry, scones, browning toppings	220–230	425–450	6–8	hot
puff pastry	250–260	475–500	9–10	very hot

OVEN POSITIONS

Bottom of oven — use for slow cooking and low temperature cooking.
Middle of oven — for moderate temperature cooking.
Above middle — for quick cooking and high temperature cooking.
Fan-forced ovens — refer to the manufacturer's directions as the models vary.
Preheat oven to required temperature before food preparation.
Cooking temperatures and times are a guide only as ovens may vary.

SCONES, GEMS & PIKELETS

My favourite recipe is the Scone recipe, in particular cheese scones, which my dad used to make in a flash using this recipe. He tried to improve it himself but kept going back to the Edmonds recipe!

ALISON REDWOOD, GLENFIELD, AUCKLAND

When my Mum was in hospital, about 43 years ago, Dad was looking after us (six kids). At the time Mum didn't have an Edmonds' cookbook (she had always wanted one but money was tight). Dad decided he was going to make some scones and couldn't find a recipe so he went off to the shop and purchased an Edmonds Cookery Book. Of course, when he went to get the ingredients out he found the recipe that Mum always used on the Edmonds Baking Powder tin!

JOAN MACBETH, PATEA

When I was seven years old my grandmother helped me make scones to enter in the school fair. What a great surprise it was to be the winner and to get two shillings and sixpence as the prize. After that, we always called our scones 'two and six pieces'.

GORDON BANFIELD, PAIHIA

There is something magical about my old Edmonds Cookery Book. It was passed down to me by my father and my favourite memory is of standing on a stool at the age of four mixing scones from the Edmonds book. I've had lots of fancy scone recipes go through my hands over the years but I still prefer the good old plain Edmonds one. Now my dad isn't around anymore, but my children know what it is like to stand on a stool with Dad and mix Edmonds scones. Nothing can replace memories like that.

TANIA JOLL, INVERCARGILL

My favourite classic Edmonds recipe would have to be the Sultana Scones. My grandmother made them for me all the time when I was a little girl — and she made them to her secret recipe. As I grew up I found my own 'secret recipe' that she adored and said they tasted just like hers — so I wonder if her secret recipe was from the covers of an Edmonds cookbook as well! Either way, these scones remind me not only of my grandmother but also of my childhood.

SUE GINSBERG, GLEN EDEN, AUCKLAND

I recall as a young primary student making a batch of plain scones for a competition at the school gala. Sadly they weren't 'sure to rise' as I had omitted a most important ingredient: Edmonds baking powder. My father, who was a master baker, quickly came to my cries of despair and made another batch for me as entry time was near closing. We often joked about the result as my father's family bakery was always held in high esteem, but he received second prize!

JEAN HUTCHINS, TARADALE, NAPIER

SCONES

3 cups Edmonds standard grade flour
6 teaspoons Edmonds baking powder
¼ teaspoon salt

75 g butter, chopped
1 to 1½ cups milk, approximately
extra milk to brush

Preheat oven to 220°C. Lightly dust a baking tray with flour. Sift flour, baking powder and salt into a large bowl. Cut butter into flour until it resembles fine breadcrumbs. Add milk and mix quickly to a soft dough with a knife. (These two steps can be done in the food processor.) Knead a few times, then transfer dough to the baking tray. Press dough into a rectangle about 3 cm thick. Cut into 9 equal pieces. Leave a 2 cm space between scones. Brush tops with milk. Bake for 10 minutes until golden.

CHEESE SCONES
Add ¾ cup grated cheddar cheese to flour after cutting in the butter.

CURRANT SCONES
Add ¾ cup currants to the flour after cutting in the butter.

DATE SCONES
Add ¾ cup chopped dates, 1 tablespoon sugar and ½ teaspoon cinnamon to flour after cutting in the butter.

SULTANA SCONES
Add ¾ cup sultanas to the flour after cutting in the butter.

No matter how many other recipes for scones I try I always come back to my trusty Edmonds book because they are the best.

KAY

You can't beat a classic tried and true recipe for Cheese Scones — a winner every time.

JUANITA, WELLINGTON

SCONES ARE BELIEVED TO HAVE ORIGINATED IN SCOTLAND AND ARE CLOSELY RELATED TO THE GRIDDLE BAKED FLAT BREAD KNOWN AS BANNOCK. THE GAELIC 'SGONN' MEANS 'A SHAPELESS MASS'; GERMAN 'SCHÖNBROT' MEANS 'BEAUTIFUL BREAD'; AND THE DUTCH 'SCOONBROT' MEANS 'FINE WHITE BREAD'.

ALL RECIPES in this book containing
Baking Powder have been tested with

EDMONDS'

"SURE TO RISE"

BAKING POWDER

and we do not guarantee success unless
"SURE TO RISE" is used.

ALL BAKING POWDERS ARE NOT MADE ALIKE

Our Cookery Book is your guide.   Post free
on application to

Edmonds' Baking Powder,

Box 472 CHRISTCHURCH.

SCONES. FROM EDMONDS COOKERY BOOK, 24TH DE LUXE EDITION (1987).

FROM EDMONDS COOKERY BOOK, 4TH EDITION.

GIRDLE SCONES

MAKES 8

1 cup Edmonds standard grade flour
1 teaspoon Edmonds baking powder
⅛ teaspoon salt

1 tablespoon butter
milk to mix

Sift dry ingredients. Rub in butter. Add sufficient milk to make a fairly soft dough. Roll out fairly thin, make into a round, and cut into eight. Cook on a hot greased girdle 5 minutes on each side.

Girdle Scones have been made throughout two generations of my family — my grandmother and mother — and are now made by me, who will in turn teach them to our son as he gets a little older. I still use the handed-down deluxe edition of the third printing in 1957.

NOELLE BYERS, QUEENSTOWN

CHELSEA BUNS

MAKES 10

1 tablespoon sugar
½ cup tepid water
3 teaspoons Edmonds active yeast
½ cup milk
50 g butter
2 eggs
4 cups Edmonds high grade flour

25 g butter
½ cup brown sugar
1 teaspoon mixed spice
½ cup sultanas
½ cup currants

WHITE ICING (see page 69)

Preheat oven to 190°C. Dissolve first measure of sugar in water. Sprinkle over yeast. Leave for 10 minutes or until frothy. Place milk in a small saucepan and heat until just before it boils. Add first measure of butter and stir until melted. Cool. Beat in eggs until combined. Place flour in a large bowl. Make a well in the centre. Pour in yeast and milk mixture. Mix with a wooden spoon until combined. Turn onto a lightly floured surface and knead until smooth and elastic. Place dough in a greased bowl. Turn dough over. Cover with plastic wrap and set aside in a warm place until the dough doubles in bulk. Punch dough down. Turn onto a floured surface and knead until smooth. Roll dough into a 35 cm square. Melt second measure of butter and use to brush dough liberally. Combine brown sugar, mixed spice, sultanas and currants. Sprinkle over the dough and then roll up as for a Swiss roll. Cut into ten 2.5 cm slices. Place buns on a greased oven tray, close together but not touching. Cover with a clean cloth. Put in a warm place and leave to rise until buns are touching each other. Bake for 25 to 30 minutes or until golden. Ice with White Icing or Pink Icing if wished. Serve warm.

FOR PINK ICING, PREPARE WHITE ICING AND ADD 2 DROPS OF RED FOOD COLOURING.

My favourite recipe is Ginger Gems, which my mother used to make in heavy oven pans. We used to put a teaspoon of butter in each shape before the mixture was put in. These were usually prizewinners at the local school garden fair.

ELIZABETH BACH, PAPATOETOE, AUCKLAND

We made gems as children and took them to Brownie and Girl Guides parties. I well recall heating my mother's gem irons in the oven and then dropping spoonfuls of butter into the pans and watching it sizzle. I have recently acquired these gem irons since my mother died but they are now a bit rusty. One of this year's resolutions is to clean the irons and make another batch.

ELEANOR BURKIN, TAURANGA

My favourite Edmonds recipe is for Ginger Gems. I remember my grandmother making these; I loved them and the smell of them cooking. We learnt to make these at school and Ginger Gems also remind me of those Manual Lessons in Form 1 and 2 and my baking practice at home.

CHRISTINE O'FLAHERTY, LINWOOD, CHRISTCHURCH

I love Ginger Gems, in fact all of the gem recipes are great but the ginger ones were tops. I'm sixty-eight and I can smell Mum's Ginger Gems in the old Atlas range even now. She had these old cast iron gem pans which were always oiled after each use. We lived in Wairoa, Hawke's Bay, and had lots of aunties and uncles living in Gisborne and Napier/Hastings. Mum could hear the sound of the car doors slamming and would have a batch of scones and gems on the go almost before the visitors got to the door.

REG CORBETT, HAVELOCK NORTH

My late mother-in-law used to bake gems all the time for the family's morning and afternoon teas. Later on I picked up a gem iron at a garage sale (I now need two) and have gone on to be the 'Gem Maker' of the family. First of all, nieces and nephews and my children ordered the 'little loaves of bread' and now they are also a favourite with my grandchildren.

TRISH TATE, HAMILTON

Mum had always made Ginger Gems and was the proud owner of a cast iron gem iron. Try as we might in early 1954 to procure one for my glory box proved impossible. I worked at Prices Foundry in Thames and when the day arrived for me to leave to be married I was presented with a large cardboard carton. I was suspicious, to say the least, as there were many pranks played on leavers. On opening it I found a cast iron skillet for pikelets, a cast iron poker and a cast iron gem iron, all made at the foundry. Joy oh joy, a proper gem iron! Over the years I have made so many and they were a huge success, finding their way to the Women's Institute, school committee meetings and the like. I still make them today, fifty years on, with my own variations.

RAEWYN APPLEBY, MORRINSVILLE

GINGER GEMS

MAKES 12

50 g butter, softened
¼ cup sugar
1½ teaspoons ground ginger
1 egg
2 tablespoons golden syrup

1 cup Edmonds standard grade flour
1 teaspoon Edmonds baking soda
½ cup milk
extra butter

Preheat gem irons in oven at 200°C. Cream butter, sugar and ginger in a bowl until light and fluffy. Add egg, beating well. Beat in syrup. Sift flour into creamed mixture. Stir to combine. Dissolve baking soda in milk. Quickly stir into creamed mixture. Put half-teaspoon pieces of butter into hot gem irons and spoon mixture into sizzling butter. Bake at 200°C for 10 minutes or until well risen and golden brown.

HONEY GEMS

MAKES 12

2 tablespoons butter
1 tablespoon sugar
2 tablespoons honey
1 egg
4 tablespoons milk

1 cup Edmonds standard grade flour
1 teaspoon Edmonds baking powder
¼ teaspoon Edmonds baking soda
⅛ teaspoon salt

Preheat gem irons in oven at 200°C. Cream butter, sugar and honey. Break in egg and beat well. Add milk alternately with dry ingredients. Put half-teaspoon pieces of butter into hot gem irons and spoon mixture into sizzling butter. Bake at 200°C for 10 minutes or until well risen and golden brown.

RASPBERRY GEMS

MAKES 12

25 g butter, melted
2 tablespoons raspberry jam
2 tablespoons brown sugar
1 egg

1 cup Edmonds standard grade flour
1½ teaspoons Edmonds baking powder
½ cup milk
extra butter

Preheat gem irons in oven at 200°C. Combine butter, jam and brown sugar in a bowl. Beat in egg. Sift flour and baking powder. Add to butter mixture with milk. Mix until ingredients are just combined. Do not overmix. Place half-teaspoon pieces of butter in hot gem irons and spoon mixture into sizzling butter. Bake at 200°C for 10 minutes or until golden.

BLUEBERRY MUFFINS

MAKES 12 LARGE MUFFINS

2 cups Edmonds standard grade flour
3 teaspoons Edmonds baking powder
¾ cup sugar
1 cup fresh or frozen blueberries

1 cup milk
⅓ cup canola oil
1 egg

Preheat oven to 200°C. Grease 12 deep muffin tins. Sift flour and baking powder into a large bowl. Stir in sugar, then blueberries. Whisk milk, oil and egg together in a jug. Add to dry ingredients, stirring until just mixed — it will look lumpy. Divide mixture between prepared tins. Bake for 20 minutes or until risen and golden. Stand muffins for 5 minutes before removing from tins.

PIKELETS

MAKES 8 TO 10

1 cup Edmonds standard grade flour
1 teaspoon Edmonds baking powder
¼ teaspoon salt
1 egg

¼ cup sugar
¾ cup milk
butter to grease

Sift flour, baking powder and salt into a bowl. In another bowl beat egg and sugar until thick. Add egg mixture and milk to flour. Mix with a wooden spoon until ingredients are just combined. Lightly grease a heavy-based frying pan with butter. Heat pan. Drop tablespoonfuls of mixture into hot pan. When bubbles appear and start to burst on the top surface, turn pikelets over. Cook other side for about 1 minute until golden.

> To the British, the term 'pikelet' indicates a small crumpet made with yeast. In New Zealand and Australia, the term has come to mean a small drop scone made without yeast. The origin seems to be from the Welsh 'bara pyglyd' (pronounced puglud), meaning 'pitchy bread'. These were little dark breads, scones or pancakes made from buckwheat flour and eaten for tea.

My favourite recipe (and my kids') is the Pikelets recipe. I love all the Edmonds recipes and it's my main recipe book. It also gives me lovely childhood memories from when my mum used to use the recipes and I loved looking at the pictures.

SUSAN

BISCUITS

200 g butter, softened
½ cup sugar
1¼ cups Edmonds standard grade flour
¼ cup cocoa
2 cups cornflakes

CHOCOLATE ICING
2 cups icing sugar
2 tablespoons cocoa
¼ teaspoon butter
¼ teaspoon vanilla essence
2 tablespoons boiling water, approximately
walnuts (optional)

Preheat oven to 180°C. Cream butter and sugar until light and fluffy. Sift flour and cocoa. Stir into creamed mixture. Fold in cornflakes. Spoon mounds of mixture onto a greased oven tray, gently pressing the mixture together. Bake for 15 minutes or until set. When cold, ice with Chocolate Icing. To make the Chocolate Icing, sift icing sugar and cocoa into a bowl. Add butter and essence. Add sufficient boiling water to mix to a spreadable consistency. Decorate with a walnut if desired.

AFGHAN SLICE
Press Afghan mixture into a greased 20 × 30 cm sponge-roll tin. Bake at 180°C for 25 minutes or until set. When cold, ice with Chocolate Icing.

Edmonds Afghan biscuits are embedded in my memory. Many Sundays Mum and I would bake these and then, when we were old enough, my sister and I were allowed to bake them ourselves. They have been a classic and a favourite in our households through many generations.

BRIDGET

My favourite recipe is Afghans. One of the first things I baked when I was a child and now my twin grandchildren are baking Afghans with me — they love them in their lunchbox. It's great to be able to pass something so easy and tasty on to them.

TRISH

My mum made the Afghans regularly all her life and they are a firm family favourite. Now that Mum has passed away it is my turn to carry on the tradition. I always have Afghans in the freezer for unexpected visitors.

SUE

ALMOND BISCUITS   MAKES 25

125 g butter, softened
½ cup sugar
1 egg
½ teaspoon almond essence

1½ cups Edmonds standard grade flour
1 teaspoon Edmonds baking powder
12 to 15 blanched almonds

Preheat oven to 180°C. Cream butter and sugar until light and fluffy. Add egg and essence, beating well. Sift in flour and baking powder. Mix to a firm dough. Roll pieces into balls. Place on a greased oven tray and press lightly with the palm of your hand. Press half a blanched almond on each. Bake for 15 minutes or until cooked.

ANZAC BISCUITS

MAKES 22

½ cup Edmonds standard grade flour
½ cup sugar
¾ cup desiccated coconut
¾ cup rolled oats

100 g butter
1 tablespoon golden syrup
½ teaspoon Edmonds baking soda
2 tablespoons boiling water

Preheat oven to 180°C. Mix together flour, sugar, coconut and rolled oats. Melt butter and golden syrup. Dissolve baking soda in the boiling water and add to butter and golden syrup. Stir butter mixture into the dry ingredients. Place level tablespoons of mixture 4 to 5 cm apart on cold, greased oven trays. Flatten with a floured fork. Bake for about 15 minutes or until golden.

I have been making these Anzac Biscuits for decades now, always a favourite!

VICKI

During the First World War, the wives, mothers and girlfriends of soldiers were concerned about the nutritional value of the food being supplied to their men. Any food they sent to the fighting men had to be carried in the ships of the Merchant Navy. Most of these were lucky to maintain a speed of ten knots (18.5 km/h). Most had no refrigerated facilities, so any food sent had to be able to remain edible after periods in excess of two months. The women came up with the answer: a nutritional biscuit. The basis was a Scottish recipe using rolled oats.

The ingredients they used were sugar, plain flour, coconut, butter, golden syrup or treacle, bi-carbonate of soda, boiling water and the rolled oats. All these items did not readily spoil. At first the biscuits were called Soldiers' Biscuits, but after the landing on Gallipoli, they were renamed Anzac Biscuits. A point of interest is the lack of eggs to bind the Anzac biscuit mixture together. Because of the war, many of the poultry farmers had joined the services, thus eggs were scarce. The binding agent for the biscuits was golden syrup or treacle. As the war drew on, many groups such as the Country Women's Association devoted a great deal of time to the making of Anzac Biscuits.

BACHELOR'S BUTTONS

2 cups Edmonds standard grade flour
1½ teaspoons Edmonds baking powder
125 g butter

½ cup sugar
2 eggs, beaten
extra sugar, to roll

Preheat oven to 190°C. Sift together flour and baking powder. Rub in butter until mixture resembles fine breadcrumbs. Stir in sugar and beaten eggs. Mix to a soft dough. Take teaspoonfuls of mixture and roll into balls. Roll in sugar and place on a greased baking tray. Bake for 18 to 20 minutes.

MALT BISCUITS

125 g butter, softened
50 g sugar
2 tablespoons sweetened condensed milk

175 g Edmonds standard grade flour
1 teaspoon Edmonds baking powder
2 tablespoons malted milk powder

Preheat ovven to 190°C. Cream butter, sugar and condensed milk together. Add flour, baking powder and malted milk powder. Roll into balls. Place on greased trays, flatten with fork. Bake 15 to 20 minutes at 190°C.

BRAN BISCUITS

125 g butter, softened
¼ cup sugar
1 egg
1 cup bran flakes

1 cup Edmonds wholemeal flour
1 cup Edmonds standard grade flour
1 teaspoon Edmonds baking powder
pinch of salt

Preheat oven to 180°C. Cream butter and sugar until light and fluffy. Add egg and beat well. Mix in bran and wholemeal flour. Sift standard grade flour, baking powder and salt together. Mix into creamed mixture until well combined. Knead a few times. Take small amounts and roll out on a lightly floured surface to 5 to 7 mm thickness. Cut into pieces of about 5 × 8 cm. Bake on a greased oven tray for 20 minutes or until set and lightly golden. Serve plain or buttered.

I remember my Labrador dog scoffing a tray of freshly baked Bran Biscuits which had been put aside to cool. But I forgave him and made another batch.

JOAN WELSH, WAIKANAE

BELGIUM BISCUITS

125 g butter, softened
¼ cup brown sugar
1 egg
2 cups Edmonds standard grade flour
1 teaspoon Edmonds baking powder
1 teaspoon cinnamon
1 teaspoon ground ginger
1 teaspoon mixed spice
1 teaspoon cocoa

ICING
¾ to 1 cup icing sugar
¼ teaspoon raspberry or vanilla essence
few drops red food colouring
hot water

FILLING
½ cup raspberry jam, approximately

Preheat oven to 180°C. Cream butter and sugar until light and fluffy. Add egg and beat well. Sift flour, baking powder, cinnamon, ginger, mixed spice and cocoa together. Mix into creamed mixture to make a firm dough. On a lightly floured board roll out dough to 3 mm thickness. Cut out rounds using a 6.5 cm cutter. Arrange on greased oven tray and bake for 15 minutes or until golden. When cold, ice half the biscuits. To make the icing, mix icing sugar with essence and colouring. Add sufficient hot water to make a pink spreadable icing. Spread the un-iced biscuits with raspberry jam and place iced biscuits on top.

> THESE WERE ORIGINALLY KNOWN AS 'GERMAN BISCUITS' BUT THE NAME APPEARS TO CHANGE AROUND THE TIME OF THE FIRST WORLD WAR WHEN ANYTHING GERMAN WAS FROWNED UPON. BELGIUM BISCUITS ARE DERIVED FROM THE AUSTRIAN CITY OF LINZ AND ORIGINALLY WERE A DESSERT TORTE — LINZER TORTE. CHANGES IN SIZE WERE MADE AND THE LATTICED TOP WAS REPLACED WITH THE SAME SIZE FOR BOTH TOP AND BOTTOM AND BECAME LINZER BISCUITS.

CHEESE BISCUITS

MAKES ABOUT 25

1 cup Edmonds standard grade flour
1 tablespoon icing sugar
1 teaspoon Edmonds baking powder
pinch of salt

pinch of cayenne pepper
25 g butter
½ cup grated tasty cheddar cheese
¼ cup milk, approximately

Preheat oven to 200°C. Sift flour, icing sugar, baking powder, salt and cayenne pepper into a bowl. Cut butter into flour mixture until it resembles fine breadcrumbs. Mix in cheese. Add just enough milk to form a stiff dough. Knead lightly and roll out on a lightly floured surface to a thickness of 2 mm. Cut into 4 cm squares or use biscuit cutters to stamp shapes from the pastry. Place on a greased oven tray. Prick each biscuit with a fork. Bake for 10 minutes or until lightly golden.

OVER ONE MILLION TINS OF EDMONDS

The following list shows the growth in Sales of

EDMONDS' BAKING POWDER

each year for the past 9 years.

In 1905	Tins Sold	..	370,600
,, 1906	,,	..	429,780
,, 1907	,,	..	502,548
,, 1908	,,	..	655,668
,, 1909	,,	..	743,796
,, 1910	,,	..	818,772
,, 1911	,,	..	878,268
,, 1912	,,	..	1,077,084
,, 1913	,,	..	1,171,344

These are big figures, but the greatest record yet broken is in the tremendous increase of the number of dainty cakes, wholesome scones, and beautifully light puddings and pastry made by the thousands of housewives in the Dominion who use

EDMONDS' PRIZE BAKING POWDER.

MERIT COUNTS—That's why we are doing the business.

36

From Edmonds Cookery Book, 3rd edition (1914).

CHINESE CHEWS

2 eggs
1 cup brown sugar
75 g butter, melted
1 teaspoon vanilla essence
1½ cups Edmonds standard grade flour
1 teaspoon Edmonds baking powder

pinch salt
½ cup rolled oats
¾ cups chopped dates
¾ cups chopped walnuts
¾ cup crystallised ginger

Preheat oven to 180°C. Beat eggs and brown sugar until well mixed. Add butter and vanilla. Sift flour, baking powder and salt into a large bowl. Stir in rolled oats. Pour egg mixture into the sifted dry ingredients. Add dates, walnuts and ginger. Mix well. Spread mixture into a 23 cm square cake tin lined on the base with baking paper. Bake for 30 to 35 minutes or until cooked. Cut into squares while still hot.

CHOCOLATE CHIP BISCUITS
(ALSO CALLED SANTÉ BISCUITS)   MAKES 25

125 g butter, softened
¼ cup sugar
3 tablespoons sweetened condensed milk
few drops vanilla essence

1½ cups Edmonds standard grade flour
1 teaspoon Edmonds baking powder
½ cup chocolate chips

Preheat oven to 180°C. Cream butter, sugar, condensed milk and essence until light and fluffy. Sift flour and baking powder together. Mix sifted dry ingredients into creamed mixture. Add chocolate chips. Roll tablespoons of mixture into balls. Place on a greased oven tray and flatten with a floured fork. Bake for 20 minutes.

> BOTH ENGLAND AND THE USA STAKE CLAIM TO THESE. THE NAME APPEARS TO CHANGE WITH THE COMMERCIAL NAME OF THE CHOCOLATE BAR AVAILABLE. BOTH BISCUITS HAVE THE SAME 'BASIC BUTTER BISCUIT' RECIPE WITH CHUNKS OF BROKEN PLAIN CHOCOLATE BAR ADDED. SANTÉ USED TO BE THE BRAND OF CHOCOLATE USED. THEY ARE NOW CALLED CHOCOLATE CHIP BISCUITS OR CHOCOLATE CHIPPIES, AS SHOP-BOUGHT CHOCOLATE CHIPS ARE USED INSTEAD OF BROKEN CHOCOLATE PIECES.

Santé biscuits . . . the best choc chip cookies ever!

TRISH

CHOCOLATE CREAM BISCUITS

75 g butter
125 g sugar
1 egg
175 g Edmonds standard grade flour
1 teaspoon Edmonds baking powder

½ teaspoon mixed spice
1 tablespoon cocoa

CHOCOLATE ICING (see page 69)

Preheat oven to 190°C. Cream butter and sugar, beat in egg, add mixed dry ingredients. Roll out, cut into shapes, and bake for 12 minutes at 190°C. When cold, sandwich together with chocolate icing.

COCONUT CRISPETTES   MAKES 32

125 g butter, softened
¼ cup sugar
4 teaspoons cocoa
2 tablespoons boiling water
1 cup Edmonds standard grade flour
1 teaspoon Edmonds baking powder
¾ cup desiccated coconut

CHOCOLATE ICING
1 cup icing sugar
1½ teaspoons cocoa
¼ teaspoon butter
1 tablespoon hot water
extra desiccated coconut to sprinkle

Preheat oven to 190°C. Cream butter and sugar. Dissolve cocoa in boiling water. Stir into creamed mixture. Sift flour and baking powder. Stir flour and coconut into cocoa mixture. Take teaspoonfuls of mixture and roll into balls. Place on greased baking trays. Flatten slightly with a floured fork. Bake for 20 minutes. Transfer to a wire rack. When cold, ice with Chocolate Icing and sprinkle with coconut. To make the Chocolate Icing, sift icing sugar and cocoa into a bowl. Add butter. Add sufficient hot water to mix to a spreading consistency.

COCONUT MACAROONS

125 g FLAKY PASTRY (see page 70)
raspberry jam
whites of 2 eggs

125 g sugar
75 g desiccated coconut
½ teaspoon almond essence

Preheat oven to 180°C. Roll out pastry and line patty tins. Place a little raspberry jam in the bottom of each. Whip egg whites until stiff. Fold in sugar and coconut; add essence. Place spoonfuls of the mixture in patty pans. Bake about ¾ hour in a moderate oven at 180°C.

DATE SURPRISES

125 g butter
75 g sugar
1 teaspoon golden syrup
1 teaspoon vanilla essence
175 g Edmonds standard grade flour

1 teaspoon Edmonds baking powder
1 teaspoon ground ginger
about 24 walnut halves
about 24 dates

Preheat oven to 190°C. Cream butter, sugar and golden syrup; add essence. Add sifted flour, baking powder and ginger. Put half a walnut inside a date and wrap a piece of dough around each date. Flatten and bake on greased trays for about 15 to 20 minutes at 190°C.

DUSKIES

125 g butter, softened
1 cup icing sugar
1 egg
1¼ cups Edmonds standard grade flour
2 tablespoons cocoa
1 teaspoon Edmonds baking powder

½ cup desiccated coconut
½ cup chopped walnuts

CHOCOLATE ICING (see page 69)
coconut, to sprinkle

Preheat oven to 200°C. Beat butter and icing sugar until light and creamy. Add egg and beat well. Sift flour, cocoa and baking powder. Add sifted dry ingredients, coconut and walnuts to creamed mixture. Mix well to combine. Place in small spoonfuls on cold, greased baking trays. Bake for 12 to 15 minutes. When cold, ice with Chocolate Icing and decorate with coconut.

GINGERNUTS

125 g butter, softened
¼ cup brown sugar
3 tablespoons golden syrup
1 teaspoon Edmonds baking soda

1 tablespoon boiling water
2 cups Edmonds standard grade flour
pinch of salt
3 teaspoons ground ginger

Preheat oven to 180°C. Cream butter, sugar and golden syrup until light and fluffy. Dissolve baking soda in the boiling water. Add to creamed mixture. Sift flour, salt and ginger together. Add to creamed mixture, mixing well. Roll tablespoons of mixture into balls and place on a greased oven tray. Flatten with a floured fork. Bake for 20 to 30 minutes or until golden.

HIGHLANDER BISCUITS

MAKES 32

125 g butter, softened
¼ cup sugar
1 tablespoon sweetened condensed milk
½ teaspoon vanilla essence

1½ cups Edmonds standard grade flour
1 teaspoon Edmonds baking powder
8 glacé cherries, quartered

Preheat oven to 180°C. Cream butter, sugar, condensed milk and essence. Sift flour and baking powder. Stir into creamed mixture. Take teaspoons of mixture and roll into balls. Flatten slightly with a floured fork. Place on greased baking trays. Place a piece of cherry on top of each biscuit. Bake for 18 to 20 minutes. Transfer to a wire rack to cool.

HOKEY POKEY BISCUITS

MAKES 22

125 g butter
½ cup sugar
1 tablespoon golden syrup
1 tablespoon milk

1½ cups Edmonds
    standard grade flour
1 teaspoon Edmonds baking soda

Preheat oven to 180°C. Combine butter, sugar, golden syrup and milk in a saucepan. Heat until butter is melted and mixture nearly boiling, stirring constantly. Remove from heat and allow mixture to cool to lukewarm. Sift flour and baking soda together. Add to the cooled mixture. Stir well. Roll tablespoons of mixture into balls and place on lightly greased oven trays. Flatten with a floured fork. Bake for 15 to 20 minutes or until golden brown.

I am a busy mum of two and we love to cook the delicious Hokey Pokey Biscuits together. My mum and I used to bake these yummy bikkies, and now I love to whip them up for my children.

SERENA, NAPIER

HONEY SNAPS

MAKES 20

50 g butter
2 tablespoons sugar
3 tablespoons honey

½ cup Edmonds standard grade flour
1 teaspoon Edmonds baking powder
½ teaspoon ground ginger

Preheat oven to 180°C. Melt butter, sugar and honey together in a saucepan. Remove from heat. Add flour, baking powder, ginger and stir until mixture is smooth. Drop teaspoons of mixture onto a cold oven tray, leaving enough room for mixture to spread to double its size. Bake for 10 minutes or until golden. Leave on tray for a few minutes to cool before removing to a wire rack.

RENEE'S KISSES

125 g butter, softened
½ cup sugar
2 eggs
1 cup Edmonds standard grade flour

½ cup Edmonds Fielder's cornflour
1 teaspoon Edmonds baking powder
raspberry or strawberry jam

Preheat oven to 180°C. Beat butter and sugar until light and creamy. Add eggs one at a time, beating well after each addition. Sift together flour, cornflour and baking powder. Stir into creamed mixture. Drop teaspoons of mixture onto a greased baking tray, allowing room for spreading. Bake for 10 minutes or until light golden. Transfer to wire racks to cool. When cold, sandwich biscuits together with jam.

COCONUT KISSES

MAKES 18

1 cup Edmonds standard grade flour
¾ cup desiccated coconut
½ cup sugar
1¼ teaspoons Edmonds baking powder
125 g butter, melted
2 tablespoons hot water

BUTTER ICING
50 g butter, softened
⅛ teaspoon vanilla essence
1 cup icing sugar
about 1 tablespoon hot water

Preheat oven to 190°C. Combine flour, coconut, sugar and baking powder in a bowl. Combine melted butter and hot water. Stir into dry ingredients. Take teaspoonfuls of mixture and form into balls. Place on greased baking trays. Flatten slightly with a floured fork. Bake at 190°C for 12 to 15 minutes, or until golden. Transfer to a wire rack. When cold, sandwich biscuits together with Butter Icing. To make the Butter Icing, cream butter until light and creamy. Add essence. Gradually beat in icing sugar, beating until smooth. Add sufficient water to mix to a spreading consistency.

CUSTARD KISSES

MAKES 20

125 g butter, softened
½ cup sugar
¼ cup milk
1 cup Edmonds standard grade flour

¾ cup Edmonds custard powder
2 teaspoons Edmonds baking powder
raspberry jam

Cream butter and sugar. Add milk. Sift flour, custard powder and baking powder. Stir into creamed mixture. Drop teaspoons of mixture onto greased baking trays. Bake at 190°C for 12 to 25 minutes. Transfer to wire racks. When cold, sandwich biscuits together with jam.

GINGER KISSES

50 g butter
½ cup sugar
1 tablespoon golden syrup
2 eggs
1¼ cups Edmonds standard
    grade flour
1 teaspoon Edmonds baking powder
1 teaspoon cinnamon

2 teaspoons ground ginger

MOCK CREAM
25 g butter
¼ cup icing sugar
3 tablespoons boiling water

Preheat oven to 200°C. Combine the butter, sugar and golden syrup in a medium saucepan. Stir over a low heat until butter has melted and mixture is smooth. Beat eggs until thick and mix in alternately with sifted flour, baking powder, cinnamon and ginger. Place small spoonfuls on greased trays. Bake for 10 to 12 minutes. When cold, sandwich together with Mock Cream. To make the Mock Cream, put ingredients in a bowl and beat with electric beater until thick and of a creamy consistency. If the mixture curdles, keep on beating until smooth.

MELTING MOMENTS

200 g butter, softened
¾ cup icing sugar
1 cup Edmonds standard grade flour
1 cup Edmonds Fielder's cornflour
½ teaspoon Edmonds baking powder

VANILLA ICING
1 cup icing sugar
¼ teaspoon vanilla essence
1 teaspoon butter, softened
a little boiling water to mix

Preheat oven to 180°C. Cream butter and icing sugar until light and fluffy. Sift flour, cornflour and baking powder. Add to creamed mixture, mixing well. Roll dough into small balls (the size of large marbles) and place on a greased oven tray. Flatten slightly with a floured fork. Bake for 20 minutes. Cool on wire racks. Sandwich two biscuits together with Vanilla Icing. To make the Vanilla Icing, place icing sugar, essence and butter in a bowl. Add sufficient water to mix to a spreadable consistency.

Melting Moments is the best recipe for special occasions and treats, and I often make a batch as a gift. My mother made me a batch fifty-one years ago for friends who were taking me on holiday to their bach in Turangi when I was seven years old.

L. GARLAND, HASTINGS

FROM EDMONDS COOKERY BOOK, 3RD EDITION (1914).

FROM EDMONDS COOKERY BOOK, 4TH EDITION.

NUTTIES

75 g butter
75 g brown sugar
1 tablespoon golden syrup
125 g Edmonds standard grade flour

1 teaspoon Edmonds baking powder
few chopped nuts
1 tablespoon milk
1 teaspoon malt vinegar

Preheat oven to 180°C. Cream butter, sugar and golden syrup together; add sifted flour and baking powder, then chopped nuts. Add milk, mix, then add the vinegar. Put out in small spoonfuls on greased trays. Bake 15 to 20 minutes at 180°C.

One of my favourite recipes is Nutties, which I remember my grandmother always having in her tins. I also make them and now put hazelnuts in the biscuits — quite delicious.

ANNIE DOELL, KAIAPOI

ORANGE CRISPS   MAKES 45

125 g butter, softened
1 × 85 g packet orange jelly crystals
2 tablespoons sugar
1 egg, well beaten
¾ cup desiccated coconut

⅓ cup rice flour
1 cup Edmonds standard grade flour
1 teaspoon Edmonds baking powder
⅛ teaspoon salt

Preheat oven to 180°C. Beat butter, jelly crystals and sugar until creamy. Add egg. Combine coconut, rice flour, flour, baking powder and salt. Stir into creamed mixture. Take teaspoons of mixture and roll into balls. Place on greased baking trays. Flatten slightly with a floured fork. Bake for 15 to 20 minutes.

PEANUT BROWNIES   MAKES 35

125 g butter, softened
1 cup sugar
1 egg
1½ cups Edmonds standard
   grade flour

1 teaspoon Edmonds baking powder
pinch of salt
2 tablespoons cocoa
1 cup blanched peanuts, roasted
   and cooled

Preheat oven to 180°C. Cream butter and sugar until light and fluffy. Add egg and beat well. Sift flour, baking powder, salt and cocoa together. Mix into creamed mixture. Add cold peanuts and mix well. Roll tablespoons of mixture into balls. Place on greased oven trays. Flatten with a floured fork. Bake for 15 minutes or until cooked.

My go to is Peanut Brownies. Everyone loves them and they're so easy and quick to make.

DEB, CHRISTCHURCH

RASPBERRY DELIGHTS

MAKES 12

60 g butter, softened
¼ cup sugar
2 eggs
¼ cup Edmonds standard grade flour

1 teaspoon Edmonds baking powder
¼ cup Edmonds custard powder
¼ cup raspberry jam
1 tablespoon hot water

Preheat oven to 180°C. Grease 12 medium patty tins. Beat butter and sugar until light and creamy. Add eggs one at a time, beating well after each addition. Sift together flour, baking powder and custard powder. Gradually add to creamed mixture, stirring to combine. Divide mixture between prepared tins. Bake for 10 minutes. Combine jam and hot water. Place a teaspoonful of jam mixture on the centre of each Delight and bake for a further 3 minutes.

SHORTBREAD

MAKES ABOUT 35

250 g butter, softened
1 cup icing sugar

1 cup Edmonds Fielder's cornflour
2 cups Edmonds standard grade flour

Preheat oven to 180°C. Cream butter and icing sugar until light and fluffy. Sift cornflour and flour together. Mix sifted ingredients into creamed mixture. Knead well. Divide dough into two equal portions and form into logs 6 cm across and 2 cm in depth. Cover with plastic wrap and refrigerate for 1 hour. Cut into 1 cm thick slices. Place on greased oven trays. Prick with a fork. Bake for 15 to 20 minutes or until a pale golden colour.

Our family favourite for three generations has always been the Shortbread.

SALLY, CHRISTCHURCH

SHREWSBURY BISCUITS

MAKES 22

125 g butter, softened
½ cup sugar
1 egg
1 tablespoon grated lemon zest

2 cups Edmonds standard grade flour
1 teaspoon Edmonds baking powder
raspberry jam

Preheat oven to 180°C. Cream butter and sugar until light and fluffy. Add egg and lemon zest and beat well. Sift flour and baking powder together. Mix dry ingredients into creamed mixture. Knead well. On a lightly floured board, roll out mixture to 4 mm thickness. Cut out rounds using a 7 cm cutter. Cut a 1 cm hole in the centre of half the biscuits. Place on greased oven trays. Bake for 10 to 15 minutes. When cold, spread whole biscuits with jam and top with biscuits with holes in them.

TENNIS BISCUITS

MAKES 30

150 g butter, softened
½ cup icing sugar
½ teaspoon vanilla essence
1½ cups Edmonds standard
 grade flour

¼ cup Edmonds Fielder's cornflour
1 tablespoon chopped cherries
1 tablespoon chopped blanched almonds
1 tablespoon chopped mixed peel

Preheat oven to 180°C. Cream butter, sugar and essence. Sift flour and cornflour. Stir dry ingredients and cherries, almonds and peel into creamed mixture. Take teaspoonfuls of mixture and form into balls. Place on greased baking trays. Flatten slightly with a floured fork. Bake at 180°C for 15 to 20 minutes.

VANILLA BISCUITS

125 g butter
175 g sugar
few drops of vanilla essence
1 egg

225 g Edmonds standard grade flour
1 teaspoon Edmonds baking powder
50 g sultanas

Preheat oven to 190°C. Cream butter, sugar and vanilla essence together; add egg, then mix in sifted dry ingredients. Roll into balls; put on greased trays. Press with a floured fork. Bake 15 to 20 minutes.

 TOP 20

YOYOS

MAKES 16

175 g butter, softened
¼ cup icing sugar
few drops vanilla essence
1½ cups Edmonds standard grade flour
¼ cup Edmonds custard powder

BUTTER FILLING
50 g butter, softened
½ cup icing sugar
2 tablespoons Edmonds custard powder

Preheat oven to 180°C. Cream butter and icing sugar until light and fluffy. Add essence. Sift flour and custard powder together. Mix sifted ingredients into creamed mixture. Roll teaspoons of mixture into balls. Place on an oven tray. Flatten with a floured fork. Bake for 15 to 20 minutes. When cold, sandwich together in pairs with Butter Filling. To make Butter Filling, beat all ingredients until well combined.

> THE NAME YOYO DERIVED FROM THE BISCUIT'S RESEMBLANCE TO THE CHILDREN'S TOY. YOYOS (OR YO YOES, AS THE NAME USED TO APPEAR IN THE *EDMONDS COOKERY BOOK*) APPEARED IN ENGLISH RECIPES IN THE 19TH CENTURY AND WERE SOMETIMES KNOWN AS 'MELTING MOMENTS'.

A GRAND ADVERTISEMENT.

1. "I'm anxious, said the elephant, with emphasis
    and vigour,
    To try some remedy for the improvement of my
    figure.
    I weigh at least ten tons, you know, when only
    in my hide ;
    My waist is thirty inches—I mean feet, of
    course," he sighed.

2. "Cheer up," I said. He shook his head. " Cheer
    up," I said still louder ;
    " I know the very thing for you—that's Edmonds'
    Baking Powder.
    It makes, although perhaps you won't believe
    it altogether,
    Whatever it is mixed with quite as light as any
    feather."

3. " If that be so," with eagerness he said, " I'll tell
    you what
    I'll go and buy a hundredweight right off and
    take the lot."
    So then and there he bought up all the powder
    in the town,
    And mixing it with greengage jam, contrived to
    get it down.

4. And scarcely had he swallowed it, when,
    singular to say,
    There came a sudden puff of wind and blew
    him right away,
    And everyone who witnessed it agreed with
    one consent,
    That, for EDMONDS' BAKING POWDER,
    t'was a grand advertisement.

FROM EDMONDS COOKERY BOOK, 4TH EDITION.

CAKES

Banana Cake is the most used recipe from my Edmonds cookbook . . . the cake of choice for my birthdays and special occasions . . . followed closely by Fairy Cakes and Pikelets.

MARION LUKA, PORIRUA

Memories of eating Banana Cake filled with cream and sliced banana, date back to growing up on a farm in Nelson. It was a weekend sort of thing, when we would rustle up something comforting and yummy. More recent memories relate to this summer — I have an old recipe book with these recipes in them at our bach in Golden Bay. My offering of hot Queen Cakes after dinner on a dismal wet day was like a little ray of sunshine!

DENISE HENIGAN, NELSON

My wife and I had never had Banana Cake in the UK and had our first taste in a coffee shop in Hamilton. We had to get the recipe and the Edmonds cookbook was the only one recommended. The cake was better than the one in the coffee shop, especially with some chocolate icing. All our parents have been out and tried the cake and it is now a firm favourite in our part of Manchester.

BEN POTTS, HAMILTON

My boys (five and four) and I make Banana Cakes (and muffins using the Banana Cake recipe) all the time. We have found this recipe the best of all tried. Sometimes we add white chocolate to the mix. My boys love cooking already and especially like this recipe and Pikelets.

JANE McCOLL, TAUPO

In the 1950s my favourite cake was the Edmonds Coffee Cake — made with the coffee essence which was commonly available then. Fifty years later my birthday cake request to my mother is still the same: 'Edmonds Coffee Cake, please'. And my mother still makes it with coffee essence — an aged bottle kept especially for this purpose!

LYNLEY COBURN, RICHMOND, CHRISTCHURCH

Without a doubt, Coffee Cake is my favourite recipe in the Edmonds book, the splotchy marks on the page testify to this. When I was very, very young (probably about fifteen years) I wanted to make a cake on my own, and the choice was this Coffee Cake. It turned out well, which was most encouraging; consequently this recipe has turned into a favourite, being made over and over. I could almost make it without looking at the recipe, almost but not quite! Now that I am in my sixties I might forget some vital ingredient!

RAE MAGSON, ASHBURTON

A family Edmonds favourite is the Date Loaf. Mum has been making this for years and years. We estimate more than forty years of making this, and around thirty a year. This amounts to 1,200 Date Loaves so far! She is now seventy-six, but still makes this every two to three weeks for her (and especially Dad's) lunchtime treat.

LOUISE IRVING, FORREST HILL, AUCKLAND

BANANA CAKE

125 g butter, softened
¾ cup sugar
2 eggs
1½ cups mashed ripe banana (about 4
   medium bananas)
1 teaspoon Edmonds baking soda

2 tablespoons hot milk
2 cups Edmonds standard
   grade flour
1 teaspoon Edmonds baking powder

LEMON ICING (see page 69)

Preheat oven to 180°C. Grease a 20-cm round cake tin and line base with baking paper. Cream butter and sugar until light and fluffy. Add eggs one at a time, beating well after each addition. Add mashed banana and mix thoroughly. Stir baking soda into hot milk and add to creamed mixture. Sift flour and baking powder. Fold into mixture. Turn into prepared tin. Bake for 50 minutes or until cake springs back when lightly touched. Leave in tin for 10 minutes before turning out onto a wire rack. When cold, ice with Lemon Icing.

THE MIXTURE CAN BE BAKED IN TWO 20-CM ROUND SANDWICH TINS AT 180°C FOR 25 MINUTES. THE TWO CAKES CAN BE FILLED WITH WHIPPED CREAM AND SLICED BANANA. ICE WITH LEMON ICING, AS ABOVE.

BOILED FRUIT CAKE

500 g mixed fruit
water (about 2 cups)
250 g butter, chopped
1½ cups sugar
3 eggs, beaten
3 cups Edmonds standard grade flour
4 teaspoons Edmonds baking powder
½ teaspoon almond essence

½ teaspoon vanilla essence

GLAZE AND DECORATION (optional)
¼ cup apricot jam
1 teaspoon gelatine
1 tablespoon cold water
dried apricots and glacé cherries

Preheat oven to 160°C. Line a 24-cm round cake tin with two layers of brown paper followed by one layer of baking paper. Put mixed fruit in a large saucepan. Add just enough water to cover fruit. Cover and bring to the boil. Remove from heat. Stir in butter and sugar, stirring constantly until butter has melted. Allow to cool. Beat in eggs. Sift flour and baking powder into fruit mixture, stirring to combine. Stir in essences. Spoon mixture into prepared tin. Place baking paper over top of cake for first half of baking time. Bake for 1½ to 2 hours or until an inserted skewer comes out clean. Leave in tin for 10 minutes before turning out onto a wire rack to cool. When cold, glaze and decorate. Make glaze by melting jam. Push through a fine sieve. Sprinkle gelatine over cold water. Sit over a bowl of hot water and stir until gelatine dissolves. Stir into jam. Brush top of cake with half the glaze. Arrange dried apricots and cherries on top. Brush with remaining glaze. Allow to set.

125 g butter, softened
1 teaspoon vanilla essence
¾ cup caster sugar
2 eggs

1½ cups Edmonds standard
   grade flour
1½ teaspoons Edmonds
   baking powder
½ cup milk

Preheat oven to 180°C. Cream butter, essence and sugar until light and fluffy.
Add eggs one at a time, beating well after each addition. Sift flour and baking powder.
Fold into creamed mixture. Stir in milk. Place 12 large paper patty cases in deep
muffin tins. Spoon mixture evenly into paper cases. Bake for about 16 minutes or until
cakes spring back when lightly touched. Transfer to a wire rack. When cold, decorate
as wished.

BUTTERFLY CAKES
Cut a slice from the top of each cup cake. Cut this in half. Place a teaspoonful of
Butter Icing (page 68) or whipped cream in each cavity. Arrange wings on cakes. Dust
with icing sugar.

CHOCOLATE CUP CAKES
Omit 2 tablespoons of measured flour. Replace with 2 tablespoons of cocoa. Ice with
Chocolate Icing — make half the recipe on page 69.

FAIRY CAKES
Ice with your choice of icing (see Icings page 68–69) and sprinkle with coloured
hundreds and thousands.

ORANGE CUP CAKES
Omit essence. Add 2 teaspoons grated orange zest. Ice with Orange Icing. To make
Orange Icing, sift 1 cup icing sugar into a bowl. Add ¼ teaspoon softened butter and
2 teaspoons grated orange zest. Add 1 drop of yellow and red food colouring then add
sufficient boiling water to mix to a spreadable consistency.

QUEEN CUP CAKES
Stir in ½ cup sultanas before adding milk.

*I'm a disaster in the kitchen but I know the Edmonds Cupcakes never fail and it's a great
simple recipe I can then decorate to make my basic baking look fancy.*

GEMMA, ALBANY

BUFFALO CAKE

250 g butter, softened
1½ cups sugar
4 eggs
2½ cups Edmonds standard grade flour
4 teaspoons Edmonds baking powder

1½ cups milk

LEMON HONEY (see page 68)
LEMON ICING (see page 69)
icing sugar, to dust

Preheat oven to 180°C. Grease two 20-cm round sponge tins. Line bases with baking paper. Cream butter and sugar until light and creamy. Add eggs one at a time, beating well after each addition. Sift together flour and baking powder. Fold dry ingredients into creamed mixture alternately with the milk. Divide mixture between prepared tins. Bake for 20 minutes or until a skewer inserted in the centre of cakes comes out clean. Leave cakes in tins for 5 minutes before transferring to a wire rack to cool. When cold, sandwich cakes together with Lemon Honey. Dust cake with icing sugar or ice with Lemon Icing.

CARROT CAKE

3 eggs
1 cup sugar
¾ cup canola oil
2 cups Edmonds standard grade flour
1 teaspoon Edmonds baking powder
1 teaspoon Edmonds baking soda
½ teaspoon cinnamon
3 cups grated carrot

¾ cup (225 g can) drained unsweetened
  crushed pineapple
½ cup chopped walnuts
1 teaspoon grated orange zest (optional)

CREAM CHEESE ICING (see page 69)
orange zest and toasted thread coconut to
  garnish

Preheat oven to 180°C. Grease a deep 20 cm ring tin. Line base with baking paper. Beat together eggs and sugar for 5 minutes until thick. Add oil and beat for 1 minute. Sift flour, baking powder, baking soda and cinnamon. Combine carrot, pineapple, walnuts and orange zest. Fold into egg mixture. Fold in dry ingredients. Spoon mixture into prepared tin. Bake for 50 to 55 minutes or until a skewer inserted in the centre of the cake comes out clean. Leave in tin for 10 minutes before turning out onto a wire rack. When cold, spread with Cream Cheese Icing and garnish with orange zest and coconut.

CATHEDRAL LOAF

125 g glacé pineapple rings
3 glacé pears
⅓ cup glacé green cherries
½ cup glacé red cherries
125 g glacé apricots
125 g blanched almonds
250 g whole brazil nuts
½ cup crystallised ginger

3 eggs
½ cup caster sugar
1 teaspoon vanilla essence
2 tablespoons brandy
¾ cup Edmonds standard grade flour
½ teaspoon Edmonds baking powder
1 teaspoon ground nutmeg
¼ teaspoon salt

Preheat oven to 150°C. Line a 23 cm loaf tin with two layers of brown paper followed by one layer of baking paper. Chop pineapple rings and pears into 6 pieces each. Halve green and red cherries. Chop apricots into quarters. Put chopped fruits, almonds, brazil nuts and ginger into a bowl. Mix to combine. In a separate bowl beat eggs, sugar, essence and brandy together. Sift flour, baking powder, nutmeg and salt together. Fold sifted ingredients into egg mixture. Pour onto fruit and nuts, mixing thoroughly. Pour mixture into prepared tin. Bake for 2 hours or until an inserted skewer comes out clean. Allow to cool in tin. Remove paper and wrap in foil to store. Leave for 2 days before cutting. To serve, use a sharp knife to cut into thin slices.

My favourite recipe is Cathedral Loaf. I had tasted this, especially at Christmas time, at friends' houses and always loved the taste and visual delight. I successfully made it for Christmas and it will be a tradition from now on.

SUSAN ALLEN, CHRISTCHURCH

CHERRY CAKE

225 g butter, softened
175 g sugar
4 eggs
350 g Edmonds standard grade flour
1 teaspoon Edmonds baking powder
225 g sultanas

125 g mixed peel
125 g glacé cherries
125 g blanched almonds,
   roughly chopped
⅓ cup brandy

Preheat oven to 160°C. Cream butter and sugar until light and creamy. Add eggs one at a time, beating well after each addition. Sift flour and baking powder. Combine dried fruit, nuts and brandy. Fold dry ingredients then fruit into creamed mixture. Transfer to a greased 20 cm square cake tin that has had the base lined with baking paper. Bake at 160°C for 1–1¼ hours, or until a skewer inserted in the centre of the cake comes out clean. Cool in tin.

CHOCOLATE CAKE

175 g butter, softened
1 teaspoon vanilla essence
1¾ cups sugar
3 eggs
½ cup cocoa
2 cups Edmonds standard grade flour

2 teaspoons Edmonds baking powder
1 cup milk

CHOCOLATE ICING (see page 69)
maraschino cherries, to garnish (optional)

Preheat oven to 180°C. Grease a 22-cm round cake tin and line base with baking paper. Cream butter, essence and sugar until light and fluffy. Add eggs one at a time, beating well after each addition. Sift together cocoa, flour and baking powder. Fold into creamed mixture alternately with milk. Spoon mixture into prepared tin. Bake for 55 to 60 minutes or until a skewer inserted in the centre comes out clean. Leave in tin for 10 minutes before turning out onto a wire rack. When cold, ice with Chocolate Icing or garnish with cherries.

Chocolate Cake is my favourite because it reminds me of when my nana and I were baking and my nana turned the mixer on but then we soon realised that the beaters were still in the drawer!

JESSICA MCCARTHY, TE AROHA

CHOCOLATE LOG

3 eggs
½ cup sugar
½ teaspoon vanilla essence
2 tablespoons cocoa
¼ cup Edmonds standard grade flour
1 teaspoon Edmonds baking powder
25 g butter, melted

1 tablespoon water
icing sugar
raspberry jam
whipped cream

CHOCOLATE ICING (see page 69)

Preheat oven to 190°C. Grease a 20 × 30 cm sponge-roll tin. Line base with baking paper. Beat eggs, sugar and essence until thick and pale. Sift cocoa, flour and baking powder together. Fold into egg mixture then fold in butter and water. Pour mixture evenly over the base of tin. Bake for 10 to 12 minutes or until cake springs back when lightly touched. When cooked, turn onto baking paper sprinkled with sifted icing sugar. Spread with jam and roll from the short side immediately, using the paper to help. Leave the roll wrapped in the paper until cold, then unroll, fill with whipped cream and re-roll gently. Ice with Chocolate Icing.

CHRISTMAS CAKE 2

225 g butter, softened
1 cup sugar
1 teaspoon almond essence
½ teaspoon lemon essence
1 teaspoon cinnamon
1 teaspoon mixed spice

¼ teaspoon nutmeg
6 eggs
400 g Edmonds high grade flour
1½ kg mixed fruit
450 g tin crushed pineapple, drained
¼ cup sherry or brandy

Line a 23 cm square tin with one layer of brown paper and two layers of baking paper. Preheat oven to 150°C. Cream butter and sugar, then add essences, spices and eggs one at a time beating well after each addition. Mix flour with fruit. Stir fruit and pineapple into creamed mixture, add brandy and mix well. Transfer mixture to prepared tin. Lay a piece of brown paper on top of the cake. Bake for 2½ hours. Remove paper and bake for a further 30 minutes to 1 hour, or until a skewer inserted in the centre of the cake comes out clean. Cool in tin. Store in an airtight container. This cake is best made 4 to 6 weeks before required.

CHRISTMAS CAKE 3

450 g butter, softened
1½ cups sugar
8 eggs
200 g sultanas
150 g currants
125 g raisins
125 g glacé cherries
125 g blanched almonds

4 cups Edmonds high grade flour
2 teaspoons Edmonds baking powder
1 teaspoon almond essence
¼ cup brandy

ALMOND ICING and ROYAL ICING
(see page 68–69, or purchased)

Line a 23 cm square cake tin with one layer of brown paper and two layers of baking paper. Preheat oven to 150°C. Beat butter and sugar until light and creamy. Add eggs one at a time, beating well after each addition. Combine dried fruit and almonds in a bowl. Dredge with ¼ cup of the flour. Sift remaining flour and baking powder. Fold flour into creamed mixture. Fold in fruit, almond essence and brandy. Transfer mixture to prepared tin. Lay a piece of brown paper on top of the cake. Bake for 3 hours, remove paper and bake for a further 1 hour or until a skewer inserted in the centre of the cake comes out clean. Cool in tin. Store in an airtight container. This cake is best made 4 to 6 weeks before required. If desired, ice cake with Almond Icing and Royal Icing.

IN PREVIOUS EDITIONS THERE WERE THREE CHRISTMAS CAKE RECIPES INCLUDED BUT WE HAVE CHOSEN TO LIST THE TWO MOST POPULAR CHRISTMAS CAKE RECIPES.

2 eggs
¼ cup sugar
2 teaspoons golden syrup
6 tablespoons Edmonds standard
    grade flour

1 teaspoon Edmonds baking powder
½ teaspoon Edmonds baking soda
1 teaspoon cinnamon
½ teaspoon ground ginger
whipped cream to serve

Preheat oven to 200°C. Grease 12 sponge oyster or shallow patty tins. Beat eggs and sugar until thick. Add golden syrup and beat well. Sift together flour, baking powder, baking soda, cinnamon and ginger. Fold dry ingredients into egg mixture. Spoon small amounts of mixture into prepared tins. Bake for 10 to 12 minutes or until the surface springs back when lightly touched. Transfer to wire racks to cool. Just before serving, cut oysters open horizontally with a sharp knife and fill with whipped cream.

COBURG CAKES

125 g butter, softened
½ cup sugar
2 teaspoons golden syrup
2 eggs, beaten
¼ cup milk
1 cup Edmonds standard grade flour
¼ cup Edmonds Fielder's cornflour

½ teaspoon baking soda
½ teaspoon ground nutmeg
1 teaspoon ground ginger
pinch of mixed spice
whipped cream to fill
icing sugar to dust

Preheat oven to 200°C. Line 12 muffin tins with paper cases. Grease. Cream butter, sugar and golden syrup. Combine eggs and milk. Sift dry ingredients. Fold egg mixture and dry ingredients alternately into creamed mixture. Bake at 200°C for 15 minutes. When cold, cut the top off each cake and fill with whipped cream. Replace top and dust with icing sugar.

COCONUT LAYER CAKE

125 g butter, softened
125 g sugar
1 cup Edmonds standard grade flour
1 teaspoon Edmonds baking powder
½ cup coconut
3 eggs, beaten

FILLING
grated rind and juice of 1 lemon
1 cup icing sugar
1 egg, beaten
¾ cup desiccated coconut

Preheat oven to 200°C. Grease and line the bases of two 18-cm round baking tins. Cream butter and sugar. Sift flour and baking powder. Stir in coconut. Mix eggs and dry ingredients alternately into creamed mixture. Transfer to prepared tins. Bake at 190°C for 20 minutes. Transfer cakes to a wire rack to cool. When cold, sandwich cakes together with filling. To make the filling, combine lemon rind and juice, icing sugar and egg in a saucepan. Stir over a low heat until mixture thickens. Stir in coconut.

COFFEE CAKE

250 g butter, softened
1½ cups caster sugar
3 eggs
2 cups Edmonds standard grade flour
2 teaspoons Edmonds baking powder

2 tablespoons coffee and chicory essence
¾ cup milk

COFFEE ICING (see page 69)

Preheat oven to 180°C. Cream butter and sugar until light and fluffy. Add eggs one at a time, beating well after each addition. Sift together flour and baking powder. Combine essence and milk. Fold dry ingredients and milk alternately into creamed mixture. Spoon into a deep 22-cm round cake tin that has had the base lined with baking paper. Bake at 180°C for 50 to 55 minutes or until a skewer inserted in the centre of the cake comes out clean. Leave cake in tin for 10 minutes before turning onto a wire rack. When cold, spread with Coffee Icing.

CREAM NAPOLEONS

175 g FLAKY PASTRY (see page 70)

FILLING
4 teaspoons gelatine
2 tablespoons boiling water

300 ml milk
1 tablespoon sugar
300 ml cream
vanilla essence

Cut pastry in half; roll out each piece. Bake for 10 minutes at 215°C. Soften gelatine in boiling water; add half of milk and stir over a low heat until dissolved. Add remainder of milk and sugar. Cool. Add vanilla to cream and whip. Combine the two mixtures. Pour into a wet sponge roll tin and leave until set. Turn on to one piece of pastry. Place other half of pastry on top. Ice and sprinkle with coconut. Cut into slices.

DATE LOAF

1 cup chopped dates
1 cup boiling water
1 teaspoon Edmonds baking soda
1 tablespoon butter
1 cup brown sugar

1 egg, beaten
1 cup chopped walnuts
¼ teaspoon vanilla essence
2 cups Edmonds standard grade flour
1 teaspoon Edmonds baking powder

Preheat oven to 180°C. Grease a 22 × 11 cm loaf tin. Put dates, water, baking soda and butter into a bowl. Stir until butter has melted. Set aside for 1 hour. Beat sugar, egg, walnuts and vanilla into date mixture. Sift flour and baking powder into date mixture, stirring just to combine. Pour mixture into prepared loaf tin. Bake for 45 minutes or until loaf springs back when lightly touched. Leave in tin for 10 minutes before turning onto a wire rack.

DOLLY VARDEN CAKE

225 g butter, softened
225 g sugar
4 eggs, beaten
1 tablespoon milk
275 g Edmonds standard grade flour
2 teaspoons Edmonds baking powder
50 g chopped pitted dates or raisins

50 g cherries
½ teaspoon cinnamon
1 teaspoon lemon essence
1 tablespoon cocoa
1 teaspoon vanilla essence

BUTTER ICING (see page 69)

Preheat oven to 190°C. Cream butter and sugar, add beaten eggs and milk alternately with sifted flour and baking powder. Divide mixture into three parts. Stir dates, cherries and cinnamon into one part. Stir lemon essence into second part. Stir cocoa and vanilla essence into third part. Transfer each mixture to a greased 20-cm round sandwich tin that has had the base lined with baking paper. Bake at 190°C for about 25 minutes. When cold, sandwich layers together with Butter Icing (see page 69).

Number 1 is Dolly Varden Cake. A family favourite for my husband's family — the cake which is brought to family gatherings, birthdays and as pick-me-ups for the bad day at work. Personal tradition is to make it two layered not three (top layer plain, bottom layer with sultanas and mixed spice added, with white icing in the sandwich layer and pink icing dusted with coconut on top).

CHRISTINA ANN (TINA) LUCAS, ASHBURTON

ECCLES CAKES

50 g butter, softened
100 g brown sugar
50 g mixed peel
225 g currants

1 teaspoon cinnamon
1 small nutmeg, grated
FLAKY PASTRY (see page 70)
sugar to sprinkle

Preheat oven to 200°C. Cream the butter and sugar. Fold in mixed peel, currants, cinnamon and nutmeg. Roll pastry out thinly and cut into rounds 10 cm in diameter. Put a little of the mixture on the centre of each, wet the edges and pinch them together to make a ball. Turn over and flatten until the currants show through. Mark the tops, sprinkle with sugar and bake at 200°C.

My old favourite was Eccles Cakes. Nothing beats the smell of fresh baked cakes and it was hard waiting for them to cool. I have been lucky enough to have two of my grandmother's 6th and 7th edition books. It's great reading the old recipes and how they were made.

SHARON FLOWERDAY, UPPER HUTT

My early memories of cooking were at my nan's house. She always had her tattered Edmonds cookbook on her wooden, scrubbed kitchen table. My mum still cooks Fruit Crumble, Fruit Sponge, Rice Pudding, Steamed Sponge Pudding and Upside Down Pudding. However, only Nan could bake that Edmond's Light-As-Air Sponge.

JAX MCNAB, WHAKATANE

My favourite recipe in the whole of the Edmonds Cookery Book has to be the Three-Minute Sponge. There are several reasons for this. First and foremost, it is a very simple and foolproof recipe that even children can and do make.

For me, this recipe evokes memories of being in the kitchen with Mum on a Saturday morning, mixing the batter, and licking the spoon and the bowl. My mother was widowed when I was six and my older siblings eight and ten. This meant that money was scarce, but the Three-Minute Sponge was affordable for us. Mum was an expert in making it versatile. We had it with cocoa or plain, but my favourite had to be the marble cake (perhaps partly because there were three bowls to lick instead of one?) with pink, brown and white swirled together in the cake tin.

Our staple birthday cake was the Edmonds Three-Minute Sponge, with the flavour the choice of the birthday person. We had it iced, and sometimes we had it split into two cake pans and joined together with whipped cream for a very special treat. I still make this recipe for my own children's birthday cakes, as I know that it will always work properly.

I even remember Mum making the recipe in a sponge roll tin, and 'icing' the cake (which had been cut into squares) with chocolate icing or red jelly and then shaking the squares in a paper bag filled with coconut to make lamingtons. This was horribly messy, but finger-licking good for a kid!

ROXANNE BRASSINGTON, PALMERSTON NORTH

FIELDER'S SPONGE

3 No. 7 eggs, separated
½ cup caster sugar
½ cup Edmonds Fielder's cornflour
2 teaspoons Edmonds standard
   grade flour

1 teaspoon Edmonds baking powder
raspberry jam and whipped cream
icing sugar, to dust

Preheat oven to 190°C. Grease two 20-cm round sponge sandwich tins. Line bases with baking paper. Beat egg whites until stiff. Gradually add the sugar, beating continuously until mixture is stiff and sugar has dissolved. Add egg yolks and beat well. Sift cornflour, flour and baking powder. Carefully fold into egg mixture. Pour into prepared tins. Bake for 15 to 20 minutes or until cakes spring back when lightly touched. Leave in tins for 5 minutes before turning out onto a wire rack. When cold, sandwich sponges together with jam and whipped cream. Dust with icing sugar.

SPONGE DROPS

CHOCOLATE FRUIT FINGERS

CHOCOLATE CAKE

FROM EDMONDS COOKERY BOOK, 4TH DE LUXE EDITION (1959).

1. BAKING POWDER BREAD   3. ROCK CAKES
2. THREE-MINUTE SPONGE   4. CURRANT SCONES

FROM EDMONDS COOKERY BOOK, 6TH EDITION.

LIGHT-AS-AIR-SPONGE

3 eggs, separated
¾ cup caster sugar
¾ cup Edmonds Fielder's cornflour
1 tablespoon Edmonds standard
   grade flour

1 teaspoon Edmonds baking powder
2 teaspoons golden syrup
1 tablespoon boiling water

Preheat oven to 190°C. Grease two 20-cm round sponge sandwich tins. Line bases with baking paper. Beat egg whites until stiff. Beat in sugar, then yolks. Sift cornflour, flour and baking powder into egg mixture. Dissolve golden syrup in boiling water. Add to egg mixture, stirring in gently with a metal spoon. Pour into prepared tins. Bake for 20 minutes or until cakes spring back when lightly touched. Leave in tins for 5 minutes before turning onto wire racks.

THREE-MINUTE SPONGE

1 cup Edmonds standard grade flour
¾ cup sugar
3 eggs
3 tablespoons melted butter

2 tablespoons milk
2 teaspoons Edmonds baking powder
raspberry jam
whipped cream

Preheat oven to 190°C. Grease two 20-cm round sponge sandwich tins. Line bases with baking paper. Put flour, sugar, eggs, butter and milk in an electric mixer bowl. Beat on high speed for 3 minutes. Stir in baking powder. Pour into prepared tins. Bake for 15 to 20 minutes or until cakes spring back when lightly touched. Leave in tins for 5 minutes before turning onto wire racks. When cold, sandwich together with jam and whipped cream.

SPONGE DROPS

2 eggs
½ cup caster sugar
few drops vanilla essence

¼ cup Edmonds standard grade flour
1 teaspoon Edmonds baking powder
whipped cream

Preheat oven to 190°C. Beat eggs, sugar and vanilla until very thick. Sift flour and baking powder together. Fold into egg mixture. Drop small spoonfuls onto greased oven trays. Bake at 190°C for 7 to 10 minutes or until light golden. Sandwich together in pairs with whipped cream several hours before serving.

JELLY CREAMS

JELLY
1 packet jelly crystals (any flavour)
500 ml boiling water

SPONGE DROPS
2 eggs
pinch of salt

2 tablespoons sugar
2 tablespoons Edmonds standard
    grade flour
1 teaspoon Edmonds baking powder

whipped cream

To make the jelly, dissolve jelly crystals in boiling water. Wet 12 shallow muffin tins. Pour in jelly. Refrigerate for 1–2 hours or until set. To make the Sponge Drops, beat eggs and salt, add sugar and beat until thick. Sift flour and baking powder. Fold into egg mixture. Drop teaspoons of mixture onto a greased baking tray. Bake at 200°C for 5 to 7 minutes. Transfer to a wire rack to cool. To assemble, turn out jellies. Spread each sponge drop with whipped cream and top with a jelly.

FRUIT CAKE

675 g mixed fruit
¼ cup mixed peel
3 tablespoons Edmonds high
    grade flour
225 g butter
1 cup brown sugar
2 tablespoons golden syrup

1 tablespoon marmalade
5 eggs, beaten
3 cups Edmonds high grade flour
1 teaspoon Edmonds baking powder
pinch of salt
1 teaspoon mixed spice
½ teaspoon ground nutmeg

Preheat oven to 150°C. Line a deep, 20 cm square cake tin with two layers of brown paper followed by one layer of baking paper. Combine mixed fruit and peel in a bowl. Dust with the first measure of flour. Cream butter, sugar and golden syrup until light and fluffy. Stir in marmalade. Sift the second measure of flour, baking powder, salt, mixed spice and nutmeg together. Add flour and eggs alternately to creamed mixture. Add prepared fruit and mix well. Spoon mixture into cake tin, smoothing the surface. Bake at 150°C for 2 to 2½ hours or until an inserted skewer comes out clean. Leave in tin until cold.

GINGER ALE FRUIT CAKE

1¼ cups sultanas
1¼ cups pitted dates, halved
1¼ cups currants
1¼ cups raisins
¼ cup mixed peel
300 ml ginger ale
225 g butter, softened

1 cup sugar
4 eggs
2 cups Edmonds standard grade flour
1 teaspoon Edmonds baking powder
¼ teaspoon grated lemon zest
½ teaspoon vanilla essence
½ teaspoon almond essence

Line a 20 cm square or 23-cm round cake tin with two layers of brown paper, followed by one layer of baking paper. Combine sultanas, dates, currants, raisins and peel with the ginger ale in a large bowl. Cover and stand in a warm place overnight. The next day, preheat oven to 140°C. Cream butter and sugar until light and fluffy. Add eggs one at a time, beating well after each addition. Sift flour and baking powder together. Stir into creamed mixture. Add soaked fruit mixture, lemon zest and essences. Stir well. Spoon mixture into prepared tin. Bake for 3 hours or until an inserted skewer comes out clean. Cool in tin.

I bake Ginger Ale Fruit Cake for special occasions like Christmas, birthdays and anniversaries. As I am preparing the tins and the mixture for this cake it always brings back memories of the previous cake I baked. This last cake, for example, brought back memories of the wonderful day we celebrated a very special friend's ninetieth birthday, and I look forward to baking many more birthday cakes for her. What I like about this cake is no matter how big or small you want it, it still tastes and looks great. I just double or triple the ingredients depending on the size that is wanted.

PAULINE OGILVY, KAITAIA

GINGER CAKE

125 g butter, softened
½ cup sugar
3 tablespoons golden syrup
2 cups Edmonds standard grade flour
1 teaspoon Edmonds baking powder
1 teaspoon ground ginger
1 teaspoon mixed spice
2 eggs, beaten

¼ cup chopped crystallised ginger
¼ cup chopped walnuts
¼ cup sultanas
1 teaspoon Edmonds baking soda
1 cup milk

WHITE ICING (see page 69)
chopped crystallised ginger, to garnish

Preheat oven to 180°C. Grease a 20 cm square cake tin and line base with baking paper. Cream butter, sugar and golden syrup until light and fluffy. Sift flour, baking powder, ground ginger and mixed spice together. Add sifted dry ingredients to creamed mixture alternately with beaten eggs. Stir in chopped ginger, walnuts and sultanas. Dissolve baking soda in the milk and stir into mixture. Pour mixture into prepared tin. Bake for 35 minutes. Leave in tin for 10 minutes before turning onto a wire rack. When cold, spread with White Icing. Garnish with crystallised ginger.

GINGERBREAD

125 g butter, softened
½ cup sugar
1 cup golden syrup
1 egg
2½ cups Edmonds standard
   grade flour

¼ teaspoon salt
1½ teaspoons Edmonds baking soda
1½ teaspoons ground ginger
1 teaspoon cinnamon
1 cup water

Preheat oven to 180°C. Cream butter and sugar until light and fluffy. Warm syrup slightly until runny. Beat into creamed mixture. Add egg. Beat well. Sift flour, salt, baking soda, ginger and cinnamon together. Stir into creamed mixture alternately with water. Pour mixture into a greased and lined 20 cm square cake tin. Bake at 180°C for 45 to 60 minutes. Leave in tin for 10 minutes before turning out onto a wire rack.

KHAKI CAKE

125 g butter, softened
125 g sugar
1 tablespoon cocoa
2 or 3 tablespoons boiling water
2 eggs

125 g Edmonds standard grade flour
1 teaspoon Edmonds baking powder
1 tablespoon coconut

CHOCOLATE ICING (see page 69)

Preheat oven to 190°C. Cream butter and sugar, add cocoa which has been mixed to a smooth paste with the boiling water. Beat well. Beat eggs and add alternately with dry ingredients. Bake 25 to 30 minutes in 15 or 18 cm greased sandwich tins at 190°C. When cold, fill and ice with Chocolate Icing.

LADYSMITH CAKE

175 g butter, softened
¾ cup sugar
3 eggs
1½ cups Edmonds standard grade flour

1 teaspoon Edmonds baking powder
2 teaspoons cinnamon
¼ cup raspberry jam
¼ cup chopped nuts

Preheat oven to 180°C. Grease an 18 cm square cake tin and line base with baking paper. Cream butter and sugar until light and fluffy. In a separate bowl beat eggs until thick. Sift flour and baking powder together. Add to creamed mixture alternately with the eggs. Transfer one-third of the mixture to a bowl. Stir in cinnamon. Reserve remaining mixture. Spoon cinnamon mixture into prepared tin. Spread surface with raspberry jam. Top with reserved mixture. Sprinkle the top with chopped nuts. Bake for 50 minutes or until cake springs back when lightly touched. Leave in tin for 10 minutes before turning onto a wire rack.

LAMINGTONS

225 g Ernest Adams unfilled sponge

CHOCOLATE ICING
2 tablespoons cocoa
6 tablespoons boiling water
25 g butter, melted

2¼ cups icing sugar
¼ teaspoon vanilla essence
desiccated coconut
whipped cream and maraschino cherries,
   to garnish

Purchase sponge the day before required. Cut sponge into 4 cm squares. To make icing, dissolve cocoa in boiling water and combine with butter. Sift icing sugar into a bowl. Add cocoa mixture. Add essence and stir until well combined. Dip each sponge square in the Chocolate Icing. Roll in coconut. Leave to dry. Just before serving, garnish each Lamington with whipped cream and a maraschino cherry.

MADEIRA CAKE

250 g butter, softened
1 cup sugar
4 eggs
2 teaspoons grated lemon zest

2¼ cups Edmonds standard grade flour
2 teaspoons Edmonds baking powder
icing sugar, to dust

Preheat oven to 180°C. Grease a 20 cm square cake tin and line base with baking paper. Cream butter and sugar until light and fluffy. Add eggs one at a time, beating well after each addition. Stir in lemon zest. Sift flour and baking powder together. Gently fold into creamed mixture. Spoon mixture into prepared tin. Bake for 30 minutes or until the cake springs back when lightly touched. Leave in tin for 10 minutes before turning out onto a wire rack. Before serving, dust with icing sugar.

MARBLE CAKE

125 g butter, softened
1 cup sugar
2 eggs
1½ cups Edmonds standard grade flour
1½ teaspoons Edmonds baking powder

¼ cup milk
2 tablespoons cocoa
4 drops red food colouring

WHITE ICING (see page 69)

Preheat oven to 180°C. Grease a 20-cm round cake tin and line base with baking paper. Cream butter and sugar until light and fluffy. Add eggs one at a time, beating well after each addition. Sift together flour and baking powder. Fold into creamed mixture alternately with milk. Divide mixture into three equal parts. Into one portion stir the cocoa, and to another the food colouring. Leave the last portion plain. Spoon strips of the three mixtures into prepared tin. Bake for 50 minutes or until a skewer inserted in the centre of the cake comes out clean. Leave in tin for 10 minutes before turning out onto a wire rack. When cold, spread with White Icing.

ONE-EGG CHOCOLATE CAKE

50 g butter
1 tablespoon golden syrup
1 egg
½ cup sugar
1 tablespoon cocoa
1 cup Edmonds standard grade flour
1 teaspoon Edmonds baking powder

few drops vanilla essence
1 teaspoon Edmonds
   baking soda
¾ cup milk

CHOCOLATE ICING (see page 69)

Preheat oven to 190°C. Grease a 20-cm round cake tin and line base with baking paper. Melt butter and syrup in a small saucepan. Pour melted ingredients into a bowl. Add egg and sugar and beat well. Sift cocoa, flour and baking powder together. Fold sifted ingredients and essence into egg mixture. Dissolve baking soda in milk. Fold into egg mixture. Pour mixture into prepared tin. Bake for 30 minutes or until cake springs back when lightly touched. Leave in tin for 5 minutes before turning out onto a wire rack. When cold, ice with Chocolate Icing.

My all-time favourite recipe is out of my 1967 deluxe edition of the cookbook — the One-Egg Chocolate Cake. Baked in a ring tin every Sunday after our weekly roast as it seems to cook better in an oven that has been used to cook something else.

PENNY

ORANGE CAKE

175 g butter, softened
175 g sugar
grated rind of 1 orange
3 eggs

175 g Edmonds standard grade flour
1 teaspoon Edmonds baking powder

ORANGE ICING (see page 69)

Preheat oven to 180°C. Cream butter and sugar, add orange rind. Beat eggs until thick and add alternately with sifted flour and baking powder. Transfer mixture to a greased 18 cm square tin that has had the base lined with baking paper. Bake at 180°C for 45–60 minutes. When cold, ice with Orange Icing.

PEANUT CAKE

3 eggs
3 tablespoons boiling water
125 g sugar
500 g finely minced blanched peanuts

1 teaspoon Edmonds baking powder

Chocolate Icing (see pg 69)

Preheat over to 180°C. Grease a 22-cm round baking tin. Line base with baking paper. Beat eggs until fluffy. Gradually beat in boiling water, then sugar. Beat until thick. Fold in peanuts and baking powder. Transfer mixture to prepared tin. Bake at 180°C for about 45 minutes. When cold, ice with Chocolate Icing.

ROCK CAKES   MAKES 15

1 cup Edmonds standard grade flour
1 teaspoon Edmonds baking powder
50 g butter
¼ cup sugar

½ cup currants
¼ cup mixed peel
1 egg, beaten
2 tablespoons milk

Preheat oven to 200°C. Sift flour and baking powder into a bowl. Cut in butter until it resembles coarse breadcrumbs. Add sugar, currants and peel. Add egg and sufficient milk to make a stiff dough. Place in rocky heaps on a greased oven tray. Bake at 200°C for 10 to 12 minutes.

SULTANA CAKE

2 cups sultanas
250 g butter, chopped into small pieces
2 cups sugar
3 eggs, beaten

½ teaspoon lemon essence or
   almond essence
3 cups Edmonds standard grade flour
1½ teaspoons Edmonds baking powder

Preheat oven to 160°C. Grease a 20 cm square cake tin and line base with baking paper. Put sultanas in a saucepan. Cover with water. Bring to the boil then simmer for 15 minutes. Drain thoroughly. Add butter. In a bowl beat sugar into eggs until well combined. Add sultana mixture and lemon or almond essence. Sift flour and baking powder together. Mix sifted ingredients into fruit mixture. Spoon mixture into prepared tin. Bake for 1 to 1½ hours or until cake springs back when lightly touched. Leave in tin for 10 minutes before turning onto a wire rack.

TOSCA CAKE

2 eggs
½ cup sugar
¾ cup Edmonds standard grade flour
1 teaspoon Edmonds baking powder
75 g butter, melted
2 tablespoons milk

TOPPING
3 tablespoons melted butter
70 g packet slivered almonds
¼ cup sugar
2 tablespoons milk

Preheat oven to 180°C. Grease a 25 cm loose-bottomed flan tin. Beat eggs and sugar until thick. Sift dry ingredients. Carefully fold into egg mixture, with melted butter and milk. Pour into prepared tin. Bake for about 30 minutes or until cake springs back when lightly touched. Remove from oven and quickly spoon topping over. To make the topping, heat butter, almonds and sugar in a saucepan. Stir constantly until sugar has dissolved. Add milk and bring to the boil. Reduce heat and simmer for 5 minutes, stirring occasionally. Return cake to oven and bake for about 10 minutes or until topping is golden and caramelised. Leave in tin for 10 minutes before turning out onto a wire rack.

WEDDING CAKE

500 g butter, softened
500 g brown sugar
10 eggs
3½ cups Edmonds high grade flour
1 teaspoon Edmonds baking powder
4 teaspoons mixed spice
2 teaspoons cinnamon
1 kg seedless raisins

500 g currants
500 g sultanas
250 g mixed peel
250 g cherries
250 g blanched almonds
grated rind of 2 oranges or lemons
¼ cup brandy

Preheat oven to 150°C. Line the base and sides of a 25 cm square baking tin with two layers of brown paper then one layer of baking paper. Cream butter and sugar. Add eggs one at a time, beating well after each addition. Sift together flour, baking powder and spices. Combine dried fruit and almonds in a bowl. Add flour mixture and mix lightly. Fold fruit mixture, rind and brandy into creamed mixture. Transfer to prepared tin. Level top of cake with a wet hand. Cover tin with a sheet of brown paper. Bake at 150°C in the lower half of the oven, for 3 hours. Remove brown paper from top of tin and cook for a further 1 hour. (Replace brown paper over top of the cake if it browns too quickly.) Cool in tin. Wrap cold cake in baking paper, then several layers of newspaper and store in a cool dark place for at least two weeks and up to three months before cutting.

I would like to nominate the Wedding Cake recipe from the early 1960 book. I have made this several times as a wedding cake, including one for my daughter's wedding. I don't consider myself to be a great cook and would not be without my Edmonds books.

LEILA MACE, BUCKLANDS BEACH, AUCKLAND

SLICES

The recipe that I consider a classic Edmonds recipe is the Coconut Chocolate Brownies. I live about 45 minutes away from my girlfriend. We both love this recipe. Whenever she comes to see me she rings just before she leaves home and I whip up a batch. By the time she arrives they are cooked and on the cooling rack. We dust them with icing sugar and if we are feeling really indulgent she brings cream and we eat them with coffee while they are still warm.

SARAH MACDONALD, NAPIER

My favourite Edmonds recipe is Chocolate Fruit Fingers. I am no great shakes as a cook and the reason this recipe particularly appealed to me was that it wasn't too taxing for my limited abilities and, somehow, it always turned out a success. I couldn't count the times that it has been my first response to 'bring a plate' or the phone call that children or grandchildren would be down on the next ferry. I would say that a conservative estimate of the successful outcomes of this recipe would be 300 plus.

WANDA COWLEY, WAIHEKE ISLAND

My favourite recipe from the Edmonds cookbook has to be Marshmallow Shortcake because when we were growing up on the farm my eldest sister would always make this every Saturday. It wouldn't last five minutes as there were eight of us children waiting anxiously for the finished product. (Mum and Dad never got near it!)

CAROL BIGGAR, WHANGAMATA

My favourite recipe from the Edmonds Cookery Book is Loch Katrine Cake, dusted with icing sugar, rather than with icing and nuts on top. My special memories start with helping my grandmother in her farm kitchen in the early 1940s, where the Edmonds cookbook came out on every baking occasion, from feeding sheepshearers and haymakers to big spreads for friendly afternoon teas as well as a large family to feed daily. Now after forty-eight years of marriage, my own very dog-eared copy is still my favourite cookbook to refer to.

BELLE TATE, WAIUKU

ALMOND FINGERS

MAKES 10

125 g butter, softened
½ cup sugar
1 egg, separated
1 cup Edmonds standard grade flour

1 teaspoon Edmonds baking powder
70 g packet sliced almonds
icing sugar or liquid honey, to serve

Preheat oven to 180°C. Beat butter and sugar until light and creamy. Add egg yolk and beat well. Sift flour and baking powder. Stir into creamed mixture. Mix well to form a stiff dough. Place dough on a lightly greased baking tray. Roll out into a 5 mm-thick rectangle. Whisk egg white then brush over dough. Sprinkle almonds over dough. Using a sharp knife, mark dough into 10 fingers. Bake for 10 minutes until golden. Cool slightly then cut along marked lines. Transfer to a wire rack. Just before serving, dust with icing sugar or drizzle lightly with honey.

ALBERT SQUARES

125 g butter, softened
¾ cup sugar
2 eggs
2 teaspoons golden syrup
½ teaspoon vanilla essence
1 cup currants
2 cups Edmonds standard grade flour
2 teaspoons Edmonds baking powder

pinch of salt
½ cup milk

ICING
1½ cups icing sugar
½ teaspoon vanilla essence
water to mix
3 tablespoons desiccated coconut
finely grated lemon zest (optional)

Preheat oven to 180°C. Grease a 20 × 30 cm sponge-roll tin and line base with baking paper. Cream butter and sugar until light and fluffy. Add eggs one at a time, beating well after each addition. Beat in golden syrup and essence. Fold in currants. Sift flour, baking powder and salt together. Fold sifted ingredients into creamed mixture alternately with milk. Spread into prepared tin. Bake for 30 minutes or until centre springs back when lightly touched. When cold, ice and cut into squares. To make the Icing, mix icing sugar, essence and sufficient water to make to a spreadable consistency. Ice, then sprinkle with coconut and lemon zest.

APPLE SHORTCAKE SQUARES

4 apples, peeled and sliced
finely grated zest and juice of ½ lemon
1 tablespoon sugar
2 tablespoons water
2 cups Edmonds standard grade flour
1 teaspoon Edmonds baking powder

125 g butter
¼ cup sugar
1 egg, beaten
1 to 2 tablespoons milk
icing sugar, to dust

Preheat oven to 180°C. Grease a 22 cm square cake tin. Put apples, lemon zest and juice, first measure of sugar and water in a saucepan and cook slowly until apples are soft. Sift flour and baking powder into a bowl. Cut in butter until it resembles coarse breadcrumbs. Mix in second measure of sugar and egg. Add sufficient milk to mix to a soft dough. Knead until smooth. Form into a ball and wrap in plastic wrap. Refrigerate for 30 minutes. Divide dough in half and roll out each piece to fit prepared tin. Place one piece of dough in tin and spread apple over it. Lightly press remaining dough on top. Bake for 25 minutes. Cool. Dust with sifted icing sugar. Cut into squares.

CARAMEL DATE FINGERS

BASE
125 g butter, softened
½ cup sugar
1 egg
1¾ cups Edmonds standard grade flour
1 teaspoon Edmonds baking powder

FILLING
1 cup pitted dates, chopped
1 cup water
1 tablespoon brown sugar
1 teaspoon butter
2 teaspoons cocoa
¼ teaspoon vanilla essence

Preheat oven to 180°C. Grease a 20 cm square cake tin. To make the filling, combine dates, water, sugar, butter and cocoa in a saucepan. Cook gently over a low heat, stirring frequently, until a paste-like consistency is obtained. Add essence. Cool. For the base, cream butter and sugar until light and fluffy. Add egg and beat well. Sift flour and baking powder together. Stir into creamed mixture. Press out half the mixture to fit the base of prepared tin. Spread with date filling. Crumble remaining base mixture over filling. Press lightly with the back of a spoon. Bake for 30 minutes or until golden. Cut into fingers.

OTHER DRIED FRUITS SUCH AS PRUNES, APRICOTS AND RAISINS, ALONE OR MIXED, CAN REPLACE THE DATES.

CARAMEL MERINGUE

BASE
75 g butter, softened
2 tablespoons sugar
1 egg
1 cup Edmonds standard grade flour
1 teaspoon Edmonds baking powder
⅛ teaspoon salt

1 tablespoon golden syrup
½ cup brown sugar
2 eggs, separated (reserve whites for the meringue)
1 teaspoon vanilla essence
2 tablespoons Edmonds standard grade flour

FILLING
½ × 395 g can sweetened condensed milk
1 tablespoon butter

MERINGUE
2 egg whites
¼ cup caster sugar

Preheat oven to 190°C. To make the base, cream butter and sugar. Add egg and beat well. Sift flour, baking powder and salt. Stir into creamed mixture. Place a sheet of baking paper on a baking tray and press mixture into a 6 mm thick rectangle. Bake at 190°C for 10 to 15 minutes. To make the filling, combine condensed milk, butter, golden syrup, sugar, egg yolks and essence in a saucepan. Stir over a low heat until ingredients are combined. Stir in flour. Set aside to cool. To make the meringue, beat egg whites to a soft foam. Gradually add sugar, beating until stiff. Spread cold filling over base then cover with meringue. Bake at 160°C for 20 to 25 minutes. Cut while hot.

CHOCOLATE BROWNIES

250 g butter, chopped
200 g dark chocolate, chopped
2 cups sugar
4 eggs, lightly beaten
1 teaspoon vanilla essence
1 cup Edmonds standard grade flour

½ teaspoon Edmonds baking powder
½ cup cocoa
icing sugar, to dust (optional)
vanilla ice cream or whipped cream, to
  serve

Preheat oven to 180°C. Grease a 25 × 20 cm baking tin and line base with baking paper. Combine butter and chocolate in a saucepan. Stir constantly over a low heat until melted and smooth. Remove from heat and transfer mixture to a large bowl. Stir in sugar. Add eggs and essence and beat with a wooden spoon until combined. Sift flour, baking powder and cocoa. Stir into chocolate mixture. Transfer to prepared tin. Bake for about 50 minutes or until firm to touch, with cracks appearing on the surface. Cool in tin. Turn onto a chopping board. Trim off edges and cut into triangles. Arrange on serving plates. If desired, dust with icing sugar.

CHOCOLATE CARAMEL SLICE

150 g butter
1 tablespoon golden syrup
½ cup brown sugar
1 cup Edmonds standard grade flour
1 teaspoon Edmonds baking powder
1 cup rolled oats

CARAMEL FILLING
1 cup brown sugar
2 tablespoons sweetened condensed milk
2 tablespoons butter
1 cup icing sugar
1 tablespoon hot water

CHOCOLATE ICING (see 69)

Preheat oven to 180°C. Grease a shallow 20 cm square cake tin and line the base with baking paper. Melt butter, golden syrup and brown sugar in a saucepan large enough to mix all the ingredients. Mix in flour, baking powder and rolled oats until combined. Press into prepared tin. Bake for 15 minutes. To make the Caramel Filling, place brown sugar, condensed milk and butter in a saucepan. Heat until bubbling and remove from heat. Add icing sugar and water. Beat to combine. Spread base with warm Caramel Filling. When cold, top with Chocolate Icing. Allow icing to set before cutting into squares or fingers.

CHOCOLATE COCONUT BROWNIES

125 g butter
¼ cup cocoa
1 cup sugar
2 eggs
1 teaspoon vanilla essence

½ cup desiccated coconut
½ cup Edmonds standard grade flour
½ teaspoon Edmonds baking powder
icing sugar, to dust

Preheat oven to 180°C. Grease a shallow 20 cm square cake tin and line the base with baking paper. Melt butter in a medium-sized saucepan. Add cocoa. Stir over a low heat for 1 minute. Remove from heat. Stir in sugar. Add eggs one at a time, beating well after each addition. Beat in essence and coconut. Sift flour and baking powder. Stir into mixture. Pour into prepared tin. Bake for 30 to 35 minutes. Leave in tin for 5 minutes before turning out onto a wire rack. Cut into bars when cold. Dust with icing sugar.

CHOCOLATE FRUIT FINGERS

175 g Edmonds standard grade flour
125 g butter
75 g brown sugar
3 teaspoons cocoa powder
1 teaspoon Edmonds baking powder

1 cup chopped pitted dates
1 cup chopped walnuts
1 egg, beaten
CHOCOLATE BUTTER ICING (see page 68)
walnuts to decorate

Preheat oven to 190°C. Sift flour and rub in butter. Add brown sugar, cocoa, baking powder, dates and walnuts. Mix with egg. Roll out to 12 mm thick and bake 20 to 25 minutes at 190°C. When cold, ice with Chocolate Butter Icing and sprinkle with chopped walnuts. Cut into fingers.

CUSTARD SQUARES

BASE
175 g FLAKY PASTRY (see page 70)

CUSTARD
4 tablespoons Edmonds custard powder
2 tablespoons icing sugar
600 ml milk

ICING
¾ cup icing sugar
1 tablespoon boiling water
desiccated coconut (optional)

Cut pastry in half; roll each piece very thin, prick well all over. Place on two oven trays and bake 10 to 12 minutes at 215°C. Mix custard powder and icing sugar to a smooth cream with some of the milk. Heat the remainder of the milk in a saucepan. Add the custard mixture and bring to the boil while stirring. Continue to stir and cook gently for 5 minutes. Leave until cold then put between pastry.

ICING: Mix icing sugar and boiling water and spread on top. Sprinkle with coconut (optional).

DATE SHORTCAKE

225 g chopped pitted dates
juice of 1 lemon
125 g butter, softened
125 g sugar
1 egg

125 g Edmonds standard grade flour
125 g Edmonds Fielder's cornflour
1 teaspoon Edmonds baking powder

Lemon Icing (see page 69)

Preheat oven to 190°C. Put dates into a small saucepan, add a little water (about 2 tablespoons) and lemon juice. Cook over a low heat until dates are soft. Cool. Cream butter and sugar; add egg, then sifted flour, cornflour and baking powder. Knead. Roll out half the mixture and place on a greased tray. Spread date mixture over shortcake. Roll out other half and place on top. Bake for 25 minutes at 190°C. When cold, ice with Lemon Icing. Cut into squares.

ELSIE'S FINGERS   MAKES 28

125 g butter, softened
¼ cup sugar
1 egg
1½ cups Edmonds standard grade flour

2 teaspoons Edmonds baking powder
extra sugar to coat
walnuts or blanched almonds

Preheat over to 180°C. Cream butter and sugar. Add egg and beat well. Sift flour and baking powder. Stir into creamed mixture. Take heaped teaspoons of mixture and shape into fingers. Roll in sugar. Place on a greased baking tray. Place a walnut or almond on top of each biscuit. Bake at 180°C for 15 to 20 minutes, or until light golden.

GINGER CRUNCH

125 g butter, softened
½ cup sugar
1½ cups Edmonds standard grade flour
1 teaspoon Edmonds baking powder
1 teaspoon ground ginger

Ginger icing
75 g butter
¾ cup icing sugar

2 tablespoons golden syrup
3 teaspoons ground ginger

OR, for a more generous topping use:
150 g butter
1½ cups icing sugar
¼ cup golden syrup
6 teaspoons ground ginger

Preheat oven to 190°C. Grease a 20 × 30 cm sponge-roll tin. Cream butter and sugar until light and fluffy. Sift flour, baking powder and ginger together. Mix into creamed mixture. Turn dough out onto a lightly floured board. Knead well. Press dough into prepared tin. Bake for 20 to 25 minutes or until golden. Pour hot Ginger Icing over base and cut into squares while still warm. To make the Ginger Icing, combine butter, icing sugar, golden syrup and ginger in a small saucepan. Heat until butter is melted, stirring constantly.

LOCH KATRINE CAKE

BASE
1 cup Edmonds standard grade flour
1 teaspoon Edmonds baking powder
50 g butter
3 to 4 tablespoons milk
1 to 2 tablespoons raspberry jam
1 cup currants

SPONGE
50 g butter, softened
½ cup sugar
1 cup Edmonds standard grade flour
1 teaspoon Edmonds baking powder
2 eggs, beaten
4 to 6 tablespoons milk

LEMON ICING (see page 69)
chopped nuts

Preheat oven to 190°C. Grease a 20 × 30 cm sponge-roll tin. To make the base, sift flour and baking powder together. Cut in butter until the mixture resembles coarse breadcrumbs. Add just enough milk to form a stiff dough. Turn dough out onto lightly floured board and roll to a rectangle large enough to line the tin. Transfer to tin. Thinly spread raspberry jam over dough. Sprinkle with currants. Cover with sponge mixture. To make sponge, cream butter and sugar until light and fluffy. Sift flour and baking powder together. Add to the creamed mixture alternately with the eggs. Stir in just enough milk to form a smooth, spreadable mixture. Bake for 30 minutes or until cake springs back when lightly touched. When cold ice with Lemon Icing and sprinkle with chopped nuts if wished. Cut into squares.

 LOUISE CAKE

150 g butter, softened
¼ cup sugar
4 eggs, separated
2 cups Edmonds standard grade flour

2 teaspoons Edmonds baking powder
¼ cup raspberry jam
½ cup caster sugar
½ cup coconut

Preheat oven to 180°C. Grease a 20 × 30 cm sponge-roll tin and line the base with baking paper. Cream butter and sugar until light and fluffy. Beat in egg yolks. Sift flour and baking powder together. Stir into creamed mixture. Press dough into prepared tin. Spread raspberry jam over the base. Using an electric mixer, beat egg whites until soft peaks form. Gradually add caster sugar, beating continuously. Beat until glossy. Fold in coconut. Spread meringue mixture over jam. Bake for 30 minutes or until meringue is dry and lightly coloured. Cut into squares while still warm.

MERINGUES
NEENISH TARTS

COFFEE CAKE

FROM EDMONDS COOKERY BOOK, 4TH DE LUXE EDITION (1959).

PIZZA ITALIAN STYLE. FROM EDMONDS COOKERY BOOK, 24TH DE LUXE EDITION (1987).

MARSHMALLOW SHORTCAKE

BASE
125 g butter, softened
125 g sugar
½ teaspoon vanilla essence
1 egg
225 g Edmonds standard grade flour
1 teaspoon Edmonds baking powder

FILLING
1 cup cold water
4 teaspoons gelatine
1 cup sugar
1 egg white
1 cup icing sugar

desiccated coconut or CHOCOLATE ICING
(see page 69) and chopped nuts

Preheat over to 180°C. To make the base, cream butter and sugar. Add essence. Add egg and beat well. Sift flour and baking powder. Stir into creamed mixture. Place a sheet of baking paper on a baking tray. Roll or press mixture into a 12 mm thick rectangle. Bake at 180°C for 25 minutes. Cool then top with marshmallow. To make the marshmallow, place cold water in a saucepan. Sprinkle gelatine over water. Add sugar. Bring to the boil. Boil for 8 minutes. Cool. Beat egg white until stiff. Fold in icing sugar then slowly pour in cooled gelatine mixture. Beat until stiff and thick (about 3 minutes). Spread over shortcake immediately. Sprinkle over coconut or allow to set and ice with Chocolate Icing and sprinkle with nuts.

My favourite Edmonds recipe is the Marshmallow Shortcake. I have a special memory as a child standing with the hand beater making the marshmallow which had to be beaten for what seemed like an eternity but the thought of that yummy marshmallow kept me going. I have now made this for my children and no doubt will make it for my grandchildren when they come along. I therefore have to keep my old Edmonds recipe book without its cover. It is probably still the most used recipe book in my collection!

CAROL ROLAND, WHANGAREI

PEANUT SHORTCAKE

BASE
125 g butter
125 g sugar
2 egg yolks
225 g Edmonds standard grade flour
1 teaspoon Edmonds baking powder

TOPPING
75 g dark chocolate
175 g roasted peanuts
⅔ cup sugar
2 egg whites (unbeaten)

Preheat over to 180°C. Cream butter and sugar, add egg yolks. Add sifted flour and baking powder. Roll out approx. 12 mm thick and place on a greased tray. Spread with the topping. To make the topping, melt chocolate in saucepan and add remainder of ingredients. Stir until mixture boils then spread over shortcake. Bake 30 minutes at 180°C. Cut while hot.

STRAWBERRY SHORTCAKE

225 g Edmonds standard grade flour
1 teaspoon Edmonds baking powder
⅓ teaspoon salt
125 g butter

1 egg
2 tablespoons sugar
whipped cream
strawberries

Preheat over to 190°C. Sift flour, baking powder and salt. Rub in the butter until mixture resembles coarse breadcrumbs. Beat egg and sugar until thick and mix into dry ingredients. Knead, divide in two. Roll out about 1½ cm thick and press into two 15-cm round sandwich tins. Bake for 20 minutes at 190°C. When cold, put whipped cream and strawberries on one half, place other piece on top. Spread with whipped cream and strawberries.

WALNUT PRIDE

125 g butter, softened
225 g brown sugar
½ teaspoon vanilla essence
1 egg
2 cups Edmonds standard grade flour
1 teaspoon Edmonds baking powder

⅛ teaspoon salt
1 cup milk
½ cup chopped walnuts
½ cup sultanas or raisins

BUTTER ICING (see page 68)

Preheat over to 190°C. Cream butter, sugar and essence. Add egg and beat well. Sift flour, baking powder and salt. Stir into creamed mixture alternately with milk. Stir in nuts and fruit. Transfer to a greased 20 × 30 cm sponge roll tin. Bake at 190°C for 30 minutes. Cool. When cold, ice with Butter Icing. Cut into squares.

Walnut Pride has been an all-time favourite for the past thirty-seven years. When I first made it one of our friends, Bob, said it was delicious. Since then, every time he comes to dinner it is made for him — he devours quite a few pieces! I even had to make it for my sixtieth birthday two weeks ago because Bob was one of the invited guests!

ANN TURNER, GLENFIELD, AUCKLAND

FILLINGS, ICINGS & PASTRIES

LEMON HONEY

50 g butter
¾ cup sugar
1 cup lemon juice

2 eggs, beaten
1 teaspoon finely grated lemon zest

Melt the butter in the top of a double boiler or in a small heatproof bowl set over a saucepan of simmering water. Add sugar and lemon juice, stirring until sugar is dissolved. Add eggs and lemon zest. Place bowl over boiling water and cook, stirring constantly, until mixture thickens. Pour into hot, clean, dry jars. Cover with preserve covers or a lid. Refrigerated, Lemon Honey will keep for up to one month.

MOCK CREAM

100 g butter, softened
1 cup icing sugar
1 tablespoon milk

¼ teaspoon vanilla essence or
1 teaspoon grated lemon rind

Cream butter and sugar until light and fluffy. Add milk, vanilla and lemon rind. Beat until thick and pale like cream.

ALMOND ICING

2 cups icing sugar
350 g ground almonds
1 cup caster sugar

2 eggs, beaten
few drops almond essence

Sift icing sugar into bowl. Add ground almonds and caster sugar. Mix well. Bind to a firm consistency with beaten eggs and essence. Knead.

To ice cake: Brush cake with lightly beaten egg white. Roll almond icing out to fit cake. Place icing on cake and leave for 2 to 3 days to dry before icing with Royal Icing.

BUTTER ICING

100 g butter, softened
¼ teaspoon vanilla essence

2 cups icing sugar, sifted
1 to 2 tablespoons hot water

Cream butter until light and fluffy. Add essence. Gradually beat in icing sugar, beating until smooth. Add sufficient water to give a spreading consistency.

CHOCOLATE BUTTER ICING: Sift 2 tablespoons cocoa with the icing sugar in above recipe.

BUTTER ICING FOR CHRISTMAS CAKE

175 g butter, softened
500 g icing sugar

3 tablespoons wine or brandy
2 teaspoons vanilla essence

Cream butter with sifted icing sugar; add brandy or wine and vanilla. Beat well. This will keep well in refrigerator.

CREAM CHEESE ICING

2 tablespoons butter, softened
¼ cup cream cheese

1 cup icing sugar
½ teaspoon grated lemon rind

Beat butter and cream cheese until creamy. Mix in icing sugar and lemon rind, beating well to combine.

ROYAL ICING

4 egg whites
1 kg icing sugar, sifted

1 tablespoon lemon juice
few drops glycerine

Beat egg whites until soft peaks form. Gradually add icing sugar, beating to combine. Stir in lemon juice and glycerine. Keep covered with a damp cloth until ready to use. This quantity is sufficient to ice and decorate a 20 cm square fruit cake.

WHITE ICING

2 cups icing sugar
¼ teaspoon butter, softened

2 tablespoons water, approximately
¼ teaspoon vanilla essence

Sift icing sugar into a bowl. Add butter. Add sufficient water to mix to a spreadable consistency. Flavour with essence.

CHOCOLATE ICING: Sift 1 tablespoon cocoa with the icing sugar in the above recipe. For a richer icing, increase cocoa to 2 tablespoons.

COFFEE ICING: Dissolve 2 teaspoons instant coffee powder in 1 tablespoon hot water. Mix into icing sugar and proceed as for White Icing recipe above.

LEMON ICING: In the recipe for White Icing above, replace essence with 1 teaspoon grated lemon zest. Replace water with lemon juice. Add a few drops of yellow food colouring if wished.

ORANGE ICING: In the recipe for White Icing above, replace essence with 2 teaspoons grated orange zest. Replace water with orange juice. Add a few drops of yellow and red food colouring if wished.

HARD SAUCE FOR PLUM PUDDING

50 g butter, softened
2 tablespoons caster sugar
½ teaspoon vanilla essence

1 tablespoon brandy
1 tablespoon ground almonds
½ teaspoon ground nutmeg

Cream butter and sugar until light and fluffy. Beat in vanilla, brandy and almonds. Chill and serve sprinkled with nutmeg,

FLAKY PASTRY   MAKES 500 G

2 cups Edmonds high grade flour
¼ teaspoon salt

200 g butter
6 tablespoons cold water, approximately

Sift flour and salt into a bowl. Cut one-quarter of butter into flour until it resembles fine breadcrumbs. Add sufficient water to mix to a stiff dough. On a lightly floured board roll out dough to a rectangle 0.5 to 1 cm thick. With short end of the rectangle facing you, dot two-thirds of pastry with a third of remaining butter to within 1 cm of the dough edge. Fold unbuttered pastry into the middle of pastry. Fold buttered section over to folded edge. Seal edges with a rolling pin and mark dough with rolling pin to form corrugations. Give pastry a quarter turn. Roll into a rectangle. Repeat twice until all butter is used. Chill pastry for 5 minutes between rollings if possible. Use as required for savoury pies and vol au vents.

PUFF PASTRY
In the Flaky Pastry recipe above, increase butter to 250 g. Roll and fold pastry 6 times.

SHORT PASTRY   MAKES 375 G

2 cups Edmonds standard grade flour
¼ teaspoon salt

125 g butter
cold water

Sift flour and salt together. Cut in the butter until it resembles breadcrumbs. Mix to a stiff dough with a little water. Roll out very lightly and do not handle more than is necessary. Use as required for sweet and savoury pies and tarts, and quiches.

SWEET SHORTCRUST PASTRY

MAKES ABOUT 200 G

1 cup Edmonds standard grade flour
75 g butter
¼ cup sugar

1 egg yolk
1 tablespoon water

Sift flour. Cut in butter until it resembles fine breadcrumbs. Stir in sugar. Add egg yolk and water. Mix to a stiff dough. Chill for 30 minutes before using. Use as required for sweet pies and tarts.

BACON AND EGG PIE

SERVES 6

2 sheets pre-rolled flaky pastry
1 onion, chopped
1 cup chopped bacon
½ cup frozen mixed vegetables

2 tablespoons spicy chutney
6 eggs
milk

Preheat oven to 200°C. Use 1 sheet of pastry to line a 20 cm square shallow cake tin. Sprinkle onion, bacon and mixed vegetables evenly over pastry. Dot the chutney on top. Break eggs evenly over, piercing the yolks so they run slightly. Carefully lift second sheet of pastry over filling. Brush top with milk. Bake at 200°C for 40 minutes or until well risen and golden. To serve cut into squares. Serve hot.or cold.

One of the most iconic and reliable Edmonds recipes. Everyone at your picnic will enjoy it.

ALISON, BIRKDALE

PIZZA ITALIAN STYLE

DOUGH
175 g Edmonds standard grade flour
½ teaspoon salt
½ cup milk
3 teaspoons Edmonds baking powder
1 tablespoon butter

TOPPING
1 large onion, diced
2 tablespoons butter
1 cup tomatoes, fresh or tinned
125 g grated cheese
2 rashers bacon
½ cup mushrooms

Preheat oven to 200°C. Make up crust dough and roll out ¾ to fit bottom of a 23 cm pie plate. Roll out remainder of dough to form a long strip, and twist around the edge. Cook onion in butter until tender, spread slices over lined pie plate, then cover with a layer of tomatoes. Sprinkle grated cheese on top, and garnish with chopped bacon or mushrooms. Bake at 200°C for 20 to 30 minutes.

BASIC QUICHE

200 g Short Pastry or 1 sheet Edmonds
  Savoury Short Pastry

FILLING
1 tablespoon butter
3 rashers bacon, chopped
1 onion, chopped
2 tablespoons Edmonds standard plain flour
1 cup milk
2 eggs
1/2 cup grated tasty cheese
salt
pepper

On a lightly floured board roll out pastry or use ready rolled sheet. Use to line a 20 cm flan ring or quiche dish. If using flan ring, place ring on an oven tray before lining with pastry. Trim excess pastry off and discard. Bake blind at 200°C for 12 minutes. Remove baking blind material. Return to the oven for 1 minute to dry pastry out. Remove from oven. Pour filling into pastry base. Return to oven and bake for a further 30 minutes or until filling is golden and set. Serve hot.or cold.

FILLING: Melt butter in a saucepan. Add bacon and onion. Cook until onion is clear. Stir in flour and cook until frothy. Gradually add milk, stirring constantly until mixture boils and thickens. Remove pan from heat. Lightly beat eggs with a fork. Add eggs and cheese to saucepan. Stir to combine. Season with salt and pepper to taste.

APPLE PIE

200 g SWEET SHORTCRUST PASTRY
  (page 71)

FILLING
4 to 6 Granny Smith apples
½ cup sugar
25 g butter, melted
2 tablespoons Edmonds standard
  grade flour
¼ teaspoon ground cloves
2 teaspoons sugar

Preheat oven to 200°C. On a lightly floured board roll out pastry slightly larger than a 20 cm pie plate. Cut two 2.5 cm wide strips long enough to go around the edge of the pie plate. Brush with water. To make the filling, peel, core and slice the apples thinly. Combine sugar, butter, flour and cloves. Toss apples in this mixture. Spoon apple filling into centre of pie plate. Cover with remaining pastry. Press edges firmly together to seal. Cut steam holes in centre of pastry. Trim and crimp edges. Decorate pie with any pastry trimmings. Brush lightly with milk or water. Sprinkle with sugar. Bake at 200°C for 25 minutes or until pastry is golden. Test with a skewer if the apple is cooked. If not reduce oven temperature to 180°C and cook until apple is tender.

BAKEWELL TARTS

125 g FLAKY PASTRY (see page 70)
raspberry jam

FILLING
125 g butter, softened
½ cup sugar
2 eggs, beaten
1 cup Edmonds standard grade flour
pinch of salt
1 teaspoon Edmonds baking powder

Preheat over to 190°C. Line small patty tins with flaky pastry. Put a little raspberry or strawberry jam in each. To make filling, cream butter and sugar. Stir in eggs alternately with sifted dry ingredients. Add a little filling to each tin. Bake at 190°C for 15 minutes.

CHOCOLATE ÉCLAIRS   MAKES 30

100 g butter
1 cup water
1 cup Edmonds standard grade flour
3 eggs
whipped cream

CHOCOLATE ICING
2 cups icing sugar
2 tablespoons cocoa
¼ teaspoon butter
¼ teaspoon vanilla essence
2 tablespoons boiling water, approximately

Preheat oven to 200°C. Combine butter and water in a saucepan. Bring to a rolling boil. Remove from heat and quickly add flour. Beat with a wooden spoon until mixture leaves the sides of the saucepan. Allow to cool for 5 minutes. Add eggs one at a time, beating well after each addition, until mixture is glossy. Pipe 7 cm strips of the mixture onto greased oven trays. Bake for 30 minutes or until éclairs are puffy and golden, then lower heat to 120°C and continue baking for about 15 minutes until dry. Cool thoroughly. Using a sharp knife, cut slits into the side of each éclair. Fill with whipped cream and ice tops with Chocolate Icing. To make the Chocolate Icing, sift icing sugar and cocoa into a bowl. Add butter and essence. Add sufficient boiling water to mix to a spreadable consistency.

CREAM PUFFS
Pipe or spoon heaped teaspoons of Chocolate Éclair mixture onto greased oven trays. Bake as above. Cool thoroughly. Fill with whipped cream and strawberries. Dust with icing sugar.

CHRISTMAS MINCE PIES

400 g Sweet Shortcrust Pastry
(double the recipe on page 71)
(or 400 g packaged sweet
short pastry)

1 cup Christmas Mincemeat
(see recipe below)
1 egg, beaten
icing sugar, to dust

Preheat oven to 180°C. On a lightly floured board, roll out pastry to 3 mm thickness. Cut out rounds using a 7 cm cutter, and use to line about 16 patty tins. Using a 6-cm round biscuit cutter, cut out tops from the remaining pastry. Spoon teaspoons of Christmas Mincemeat into each base. Brush the edges of the bases with some of the egg. Place tops over the filling, pressing lightly around the edges to seal the pies. Glaze with the remaining beaten egg. Bake for 15 minutes or until golden. To serve, heat at 140°C for 15 minutes or until warm. Dust with icing sugar.

Christmas Mincemeat

1¼ cups currants
1¼ cups sultanas
1¼ cups raisins
1¼ cups mixed peel
¼ cup blanched almonds

2 medium apples, unpeeled, quartered and
cored
1 cup brown sugar
¼ teaspoon salt
½ teaspoon ground nutmeg
2 tablespoons brandy or whisky or lemon
juice

Mince or finely chop currants, sultanas, raisins, peel and almonds. Finely chop or grate apples. Add apples, sugar, salt, nutmeg and brandy to fruit mixture. Mix well. Cover and refrigerate. Stir occasionally. Christmas Mincemeat will keep for up to three months in the refrigerator. Makes six cups.

My Edmonds Cookery Book was given to me as a Christmas gift from my brother Peter in December 1961. I was single and had just gone flatting. I still use the book. Since getting married in 1967 I have made Christmas Mince Pies. I must confess though, that instead of '8oz apples' in the fruit mince I substitute two little tins of baby apples. I now buy frozen sweet short pastry sheets and make a dozen pies at a time. The big bowl of mincemeat lasts for several batches. My yearly Christmas Mince Pies are famous among family and friends.

Joan Gaskell, Massey, Auckland

LEMON MERINGUE PIE

BASE
200 g SWEET SHORTCRUST PASTRY
(see page 71)

FILLING
¼ cup Edmonds Fielder's cornflour
2 tablespoons Edmonds custard powder
1 cup sugar
2 teaspoons grated lemon zest

¼ cup lemon juice
¾ cup water
3 eggs yolks
1 tablespoon butter

MERINGUE
3 egg whites
¼ cup caster sugar
¼ teaspoon vanilla essence

Preheat oven to 190°C. On a lightly floured board roll out pastry to 6 mm thickness. Use to line a 20 cm flan tin. Trim off any excess pastry. Bake blind for 20 minutes. (To bake blind, cut a circle of baking paper to cover the pastry. Fill with dried beans or rice.) Remove baking-blind material. Return pastry shell to oven for 1 minute to dry out pastry base. While pastry is cooking, make the filling. To make the filling, blend cornflour, custard powder, sugar, lemon zest and juice together until smooth. Add water. Cook over medium heat until mixture boils and thickens, stirring constantly. Remove from heat. Stir in yolks and butter. Pour filling into cooked pastry base. To make the meringue, beat egg whites until stiff but not dry. Beat in sugar, 1 tablespoon at a time, until very thick and glossy. Stir in essence. Spoon meringue topping over lemon filling. Return to oven and bake at 190°C for 10 minutes or until golden.

PRINCESS CUSTARD TART

PASTRY
75 g butter
175 g Edmonds standard grade flour
1 teaspoon Edmonds baking powder
⅛ teaspoon salt
25 g sugar
about 2 tablespoons cold water

CUSTARD
2 teaspoons sugar
1 teaspoon Edmonds standard grade flour
2 egg yolks (reserve whites for meringue)
1 cup milk

MERINGUE
2 egg whites
¼ cup caster sugar

Preheat oven to 200°C. Rub butter into flour; add baking powder, salt and sugar; mix with cold water to a firm dough. Line a tin or enamel plate with the pastry. Fill with custard made by mixing together sugar, flour, egg yolks and milk. Bake 30 minutes at 200°C. Cool. Spread thinly with raspberry jam, and pile meringue on top. To make the meringue, beat egg whites until stiff. Gradually add sugar, beating continuously. Beat until glossy. Bake at 120°C until golden.

NEENISH TARTS

125 g butter, softened
½ cup sugar
1 egg
2 cups Edmonds standard grade flour
1 teaspoon Edmonds baking powder
pinch of salt

FILLING
½ cup icing sugar
100 g butter, softened
½ cup sweetened condensed milk
2 tablespoons lemon juice

WHITE ICING (see page 69)
CHOCOLATE ICING (see page 69)

Preheat oven to 180°C. Cream butter and sugar until light and fluffy. Add egg and beat well. Sift flour, baking powder and salt together. Mix into creamed mixture, stirring well. Turn mixture out onto a lightly floured board and knead well. Wrap pastry in plastic food wrap and chill pastry for 15 minutes. Roll out pastry to 2 mm thickness. Cut out rounds using a 7 cm cutter and line patty tins. Prick bases. Bake for 12 minutes or until cooked. Cool pastry cases and fill with filling. To make filling, sift icing sugar into a bowl. Add butter, condensed milk and lemon juice. Beat until smooth. Allow filling to set in fridge. Ice one half of each tart with White Icing and the other half with Chocolate Icing.

THE EARLIEST REFERENCE TO NEENISH TARTS WE HAVE BEEN ABLE TO FIND OCCURS IN A 1929 RECIPE FOR NEENISH CAKES IN *MISS DRAKE'S HOME COOKERY* BY LUCY DRAKE, PUBLISHED AT GLENFERRIE IN VICTORIA, AUSTRALIA. RECIPES FOR NEENISH TARTS EXIST IN AUSTRALIAN COOKBOOKS PUBLISHED IN THE 1930S AND 1940S UNDER THE NAME 'NEINICH TART', SUGGESTING A EUROPEAN ORIGIN. A COLUMN APPEARED IN THE *SYDNEY MORNING HERALD* IN 1995 ATTRIBUTING THE DISCOVERY OF NEENISH TARTS TO MRS RUBY NEENISH OF GRONG GRONG, WHO IS SAID TO HAVE FIRST MADE THEM IN 1913. THIS SEEMS UNLIKELY, GIVEN THE EXISTENCE OF RECIPES UNDER THE NAME 'NEINICH'. IT IS INTERESTING TO NOTE THAT THE EARLIER RECIPES USE WHITE AND PINK ICING, NOT THE WHITE AND CHOCOLATE WHICH IS COMMON TODAY.

When I was a young mother my girlfriends and I used to get together for afternoon teas with the best bone china, etc. My best friend always made Neenish Tarts when it was her turn to entertain. Every time I see them in a bakery, I am immediately back in the early sixties.

ANN ABSALOM, STOKE, NELSON

SOUPS

FRENCH ONION SOUP

SERVES 4 TO 6

3 tablespoons butter
6 medium onions, thinly sliced
1 teaspoon sugar
4 cups liquid beef stock

salt
black pepper
¼ cup dry sherry
4 to 6 slices cheese on toast

Melt the butter in a saucepan. Add onions and sugar. Cook slowly for 15 minutes or until onion is golden. Add beef stock. Bring to the boil then simmer for 15 minutes. Season with salt and pepper to taste. Just before serving add sherry. Grill cheese on toast. Cut into triangles or squares and place on soup.

One of my favourite Edmonds Cookery Book recipes when I first started learning to cook was French Onion Soup. My mum had all the best ways to teach us to cook. Because she only had four boys she would often get us all keen in the kitchen by making this soup recipe because our surname is French. So we kids enjoyed getting the onions ready and learning how to make beef stock. Mum would wander away to the 'adults-only' cupboard to get the small glass of sherry that made this Edmonds recipe that much better.

STEPHEN FRENCH

LEEK AND POTATO SOUP

SERVES 4 TO 5

5 medium potatoes, chopped
2 teaspoons canola oil or butter
2 small leeks, thinly sliced
1 clove garlic, crushed
200 g bacon pieces
6 cups liquid chicken stock
1 bay leaf

2 sprigs parsley
1 cup milk
¼ cup chopped parsley
salt
white pepper
grated tasty cheddar cheese

Cook potatoes in boiling salted water until tender. Drain and mash. Set aside. Heat the oil in a large saucepan. Add leeks, garlic and bacon. Cook without colouring until leeks are tender. Pour in stock. Add bay leaf and parsley sprigs. Bring to the boil. Reduce heat and simmer for 20 minutes. Remove bay leaf and parsley sprigs. Add mashed potato. Simmer for 15 minutes. Stir in the milk and chopped parsley. Season with salt and pepper to taste. Served garnished with cheese.

MUSHROOM SOUP

SERVES 4 TO 5

3 tablespoons butter
1 onion, chopped
500 g mushrooms, sliced
3 tablespoons Edmonds standard
    grade flour
2 cups milk

1 cup liquid chicken stock
½ teaspoon salt
white pepper
1 teaspoon lemon juice
chopped parsley or chives

Melt butter in a saucepan. Add onion and mushrooms. Cook until onion is clear.
Stir in the flour. Cook, stirring, for 1 minute. Gradually add milk and stock, stirring
constantly. Bring to the boil. Cook for 5 minutes or until soup thickens slightly. Add
salt, pepper and lemon juice. Serve garnished with parsley.

OLD-FASHIONED VEGETABLE SOUP

SERVES 8 TO 10

1 kg beef bones, fat removed
3 litres water
½ cup red lentils
½ cup pearl barley
½ cup split peas

3 cups chopped vegetables, e.g. carrots,
    potatoes, parsnips
salt
black pepper

Put bones, water, lentils, barley and split peas in a large saucepan. Bring to the boil
and simmer for 2 to 3 hours until meat is falling off the bones. Remove bones, fat and
gristle from the soup. Add vegetables. Cook for 30 to 45 minutes. Season with salt and
pepper to taste.

PEA AND HAM SOUP

SERVES 6

500 g bacon or ham bones
250 g split peas
1 medium onion, finely chopped

1 teaspoon salt
3 litres water
freshly ground black pepper

Put all ingredients in a large saucepan. Simmer slowly for 2 to 3 hours until peas
are soft. For a very creamy soup, remove bones and purée soup in a blender or push
through a sieve. Cut meat from bones and return to soup.

*My children will not eat pumpkin with a meal but I have no trouble getting them to eat
Pumpkin Soup. A large pot of this taken to after-rugby functions is always the first thing to go.*
KAREN LUKE, DANNEVIRKE

PUMPKIN SOUP

1 tablespoon canola oil
1 onion, chopped
750 g pumpkin, peeled and chopped
1 large potato, peeled and chopped

4 cups liquid chicken stock
salt
black pepper
nutmeg to season

Heat oil in a saucepan. Add onion and cook until clear. Add pumpkin, potato and stock. Cover, bring to the boil and cook until vegetables are soft. Purée vegetable mixture in a blender or push through a sieve. Season with salt, pepper and nutmeg to taste. For extra flavour, a ham hock or bacon bones can be added when cooking the pumpkin.

SPINACH SOUP

SERVES 4 TO 5

50 g butter
1 onion, chopped
1 clove garlic, crushed
500 g spinach, washed,
    stems removed
2 cups liquid chicken stock

½ teaspoon salt
black pepper
½ teaspoon sugar
pinch of nutmeg
sour cream or unsweetened
    natural yoghurt

Melt the butter in a saucepan. Add onion and garlic, and cook until onion is clear. Add spinach, stock, salt and pepper to taste. Bring to the boil, cover and leave to simmer for 10 to 15 minutes or until spinach is limp, but still very green. Add sugar. Purée in a blender until smooth. Add nutmeg. Serve garnished with a swirl of sour cream.

My favourite Edmonds recipe is for Spinach Soup. It brings back special memories of sharing Kiwi vegetarian recipes with my Indian in-laws.

EMILIE LAD, MT ROSKILL, AUCKLAND

TOMATO SOUP

SERVES 4 TO 5

2 teaspoons butter or canola oil
1 onion, finely chopped
1 stalk celery, chopped
6 medium tomatoes
½ teaspoon salt

black pepper
¼ cup tomato paste
2 cups liquid chicken stock
pinch of chilli powder or cayenne pepper
sour cream to garnish

Melt butter in a medium saucepan. Add onion and celery and cook until onion is clear. Blanch the tomatoes by placing in boiling water for 30 seconds then plunging into cold water. Remove skins. Chop the flesh. Stir the tomatoes, salt, pepper, tomato paste and stock into the onion and celery. Add the chilli powder. Bring almost to the boil. Purée in blender. Serve garnished with a swirl of sour cream.

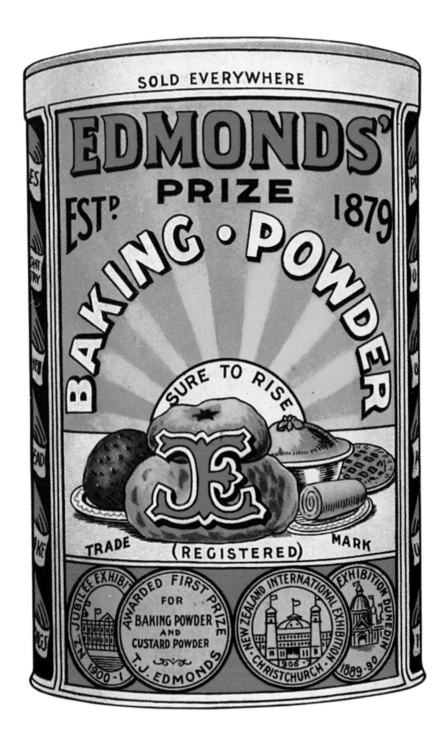

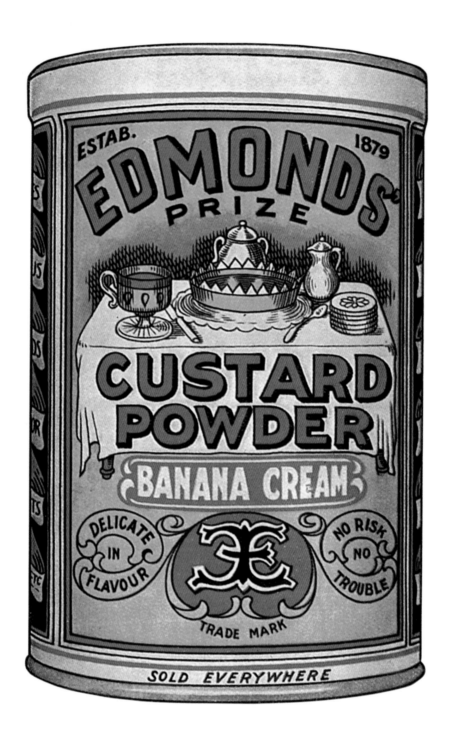

VINTAGE EDMONDS ADVERTISEMENT

FISH

My favourite recipe from the Edmonds Cookery Book is Fish Pie Supreme. We have used it often but there is a story that really makes it special for me. In late 1999 our youngest daughter was slowly making her way back to New Zealand from the UK via Canada with a side trip to Mexico and Central America. On Christmas Eve she rang us from a small beach in Belize to wish us a Merry Christmas and a Happy New Year. At least that is what we thought was the reason for the call. The real reason became quickly apparent. She and her friend had met up with some other young folk and they were all wondering what to have for Christmas dinner in their very primitive, off-the-beaten track village. In the local market she noticed some smoked fish and thought Fish Pie Supreme! So her first words to my wife were 'while we chat get Dad to get the Edmonds cookbook and read me out the recipe for Fish Pie Supreme'. We understand it was a great success and that all enjoyed their unusual Christmas dinner in a far off part of the world.

IAN DUTHIE, KARORI, WELLINGTON

FISH TYPES

WHOLE FISH: snapper, sole, flounder, blue and red cod, John Dory, hapuku, hake, hoki, ling, tarakihi, trevally.
MEDIUM-FIRM FISH: blue cod, John Dory, hapuku, gurnard, kahawai, ling, moki, orange roughy, snapper, tarakihi, trevally.
SOFT-TEXTURED FISH: red cod, flounder, gemfish, hake, hoki, sole.
FISH STEAKS: salmon, hapuku.

BUYING FISH

Look for fish that has:
- no smell of ammonia or strong odour,
- translucent, firm flesh,
- scales that are intact,
- gills that are bright red,
- bulging, bright eyes,
- no blood in the body cavity.

COOKING FISH

POACHING (BOILING): Weigh fish and calculate cooking time. Wrap fish in foil or place on a steaming rack. Place fish in a saucepan with sufficient water to just cover. Cover and simmer gently until fish is tender. Drain and serve with sauce of your choice. Suitable for all fish types.

STEAMING: Place fish in a lightly greased steamer and cook until done. Suitable for all fish types.

GRILLING: Heat the grill. Lightly grease the grilling rack. Remove head, fins and tail from whole fish. Cut slashes in the flesh of thick fish to allow heat to penetrate. Brush with melted butter or oil. During cooking time brush again with melted butter or oil. Suitable for all fish types.

BAKING: Remove fins from fish. Weigh fish and calculate the cooking time. Stuff fish cavity if wished. Close opening with small skewers laced together with fine string or sew opening together with a needle and coarse thread. Place fish in a greased baking dish or roasting pan. Brush with melted butter or oil and bake at 180°C until cooked. Suitable for all fish types.

FRYING: Wipe fish and cut into serving-sized pieces if wished. Fry in hot oil until golden and cooked. Drain fish on absorbent paper. Suitable for all fish types.
Pan frying — dust with seasoned flour.
Shallow or deep frying — dip in egg and coat in breadcrumbs. Alternatively dust with seasoned flour and coat with batter.

COOKING TIMES FOR FISH

Cooking times are a guide only and are dependent on the size and thickness of the fish.

POACHED OR STEAMED:	whole —	10 to 15 minutes per 500 g
	fillets —	4 to 6 minutes per 500 g
GRILLING:	whole —	10 to 13 minutes per 500 g
	fillets —	4 to 8 minutes per 500 g
BAKING:	whole —	30 minutes per 500 g
	fillets —	10 to 15 minutes per 500 g
MICROWAVING:	whole or	
	fillets —	1 minute per 100 g on full power 5 minutes per 500 g on full power

TO TEST FOR DONENESS

Fish is cooked when the flesh flakes easily, or when the flesh separates from the bones, or when a creamy white juice comes from the flesh.

BEER BATTER   MAKES ABOUT 1 CUP

½ cup Edmonds standard grade flour   ¼ cup beer, approximately
½ teaspoon salt

Sift flour and salt into bowl. Add measure of beer without a head. Mix to a smooth batter.

KEDGEREE

1½ cups long grain rice
2 tablespoons butter
1 large onion, finely chopped
250 g smoked fish, flaked
2 tablespoons chopped parsley

2 tablespoons lemon juice
salt and freshly ground black pepper to
  season
4 hard-boiled eggs, shelled and quartered

Place rice in a sieve. Wash under cold running water to remove starch. Cook in boiling water for 12 minutes until tender. Tip into sieve and rinse under cold running water to cool. Drain thoroughly. Spread rice in a thin layer over the base of a baking dish. Set aside for 1 hour to allow rice to dry. Melt butter in a heavy-based frying pan. Cook onion for 5 minutes until soft. Add rice and fish, tossing until heated through. Remove from heat. Stir in parsley and lemon juice. Season. Gently fold egg quarters through the rice mixture.

FISH PIE SUPREME

25 g butter
1 tablespoon milk
3 cups cooked mashed potatoes
½ teaspoon salt
black pepper
1 tablespoon butter

1 tablespoon Edmonds standard grade flour
1 cup milk
500 g smoked fish, flaked or 425 g can
  tuna, drained and flaked
1 tablespoon chopped parsley
2 hard-boiled eggs, chopped

Preheat oven to 190°C. Mash cooked potatoes with first measure of butter and milk, beating with a fork to combine. Season with salt and pepper to taste. Line a 20 cm pie dish with half the potatoes. Set remaining potatoes aside. Heat second measure of butter in a saucepan. Stir in flour and cook until frothy. Gradually add second measure of milk, stirring constantly until sauce boils and thickens. Remove from heat. Add fish, parsley and eggs. Pour this mixture into the lined pie dish. Cover with remaining potato. Cook at 190°C for 20 minutes or until pale golden.

SALMON RISSOLES

210 g can salmon, drained
1 cup mashed potato
1 cup Edmonds standard grade flour
2 teaspoons Edmonds baking powder

salt and pepper
1 tablespoon chopped parsley
cooking oil to cook

Combine all ingredients (except oil) in a bowl. Form into small flat rissoles. Pour sufficient oil over the base of a frying pan to cover. Heat. Add rissoles and cook over a medium heat until golden. Drain on paper towels. A grated onion may be added if desired.

TUNA FISH PIE

2 tablespoons butter
1 chicken stock cube
2 tablespoons Edmonds standard
  grade flour
2 cups milk
1 teaspoon Worcestershire sauce

1 tablespoon sherry (optional)
2 tablespoons chopped parsley
salt and freshly ground black pepper to
  season
2 × 225 g cans tuna, drained and flaked
225 g SHORT PASTRY (see page 70)

Preheat oven to 215°C. Make a white sauce by melting butter in a small saucepan.
Crumble stock cube with flour and add to butter, stirring over a low heat for 1 minute.
Remove pan from heat. Gradually add milk, stirring constantly. Return pan to heat. Stir
over a medium heat until sauce thickens and comes to the boil. Simmer for 5 minutes.
Remove from heat. Stir in Worcestershire sauce, sherry, parsley and salt and pepper.
Gently fold through tuna. Transfer to an ovenproof dish. Roll pastry out to a thickness of
5 mm. Place over fish mixture, trimming off excess. Bake at 215°C for 15 to 20 minutes or
until golden. Optional additions: chopped celery, chopped onion, sliced hard-boiled egg.

TUNA RICE BAKE

SERVES 4

¾ cup long grain rice
2 tablespoons butter
1 clove garlic, crushed
1 onion, sliced
2 stalks celery, sliced
1 tablespoon Edmonds standard grade flour

1 cup milk
2 eggs, beaten
½ cup grated tasty cheddar cheese
2 tablespoons chopped parsley
425 g can tuna, drained and flaked
salt and freshly ground black pepper

Preheat oven to 180°C. Place rice in a sieve. Wash under cold running water to remove
starch. Cook rice in boiling water for 12 minutes until tender. Transfer to a sieve.
Rinse under cold running water to cool. Drain thoroughly. Melt butter in a saucepan.
Add garlic, onion and celery. Cook for 5 minutes until onion is soft. Add flour and stir
constantly for 2 minutes. Remove from heat. Gradually add milk, stirring constantly.
Return pan to heat, stirring continuously until sauce thickens and comes to the
boil. Remove from heat. Add eggs and half the cheese. Mix well. Stir in cooked rice,
then parsley and tuna. Season to taste. Transfer mixture to a greased ovenproof
dish. Sprinkle with remaining cheese. Cook at 180°C for 20 minutes or until golden.
Serve hot or cold.

WHITEBAIT FRITTERS

SERVES 4 TO 6

1 cup Edmonds standard grade flour
½ teaspoon Edmonds baking powder
½ teaspoon salt
1 egg
½ cup milk, approximately

125 g whitebait or strips of firm white fish,
   e.g. lemon fish, trevally, orange roughy
Amco cooking oil for shallow frying
lemon wedges

Sift flour, baking powder and salt into a bowl. Add egg and sufficient milk to mix to a smooth batter. Drain whitebait well. Stir in whitebait or fish. Coat well with egg mixture. Heat oil in a large frying pan. Add fritters and cook until golden on both sides. Drain on absorbent paper. Serve with lemon.

WHITEBAIT FRITTERS 2

500 g whitebait
1 tablespoon Edmonds standard
   grade flour
4 teaspoons milk

1 egg, separated
pepper and salt
2 teaspoons chopped parsley
cooking oil for frying

Wash and dry whitebait. Mix flour to a smooth paste with milk and beaten egg yolk. Add salt, pepper and parsley. Beat egg white until stiff, add flour mixture and whitebait. Shallow fry in hot oil until golden brown. Drain on brown paper. Serve garnished with parsley or lemon.

MOCK WHITEBAIT PATTIES

1 egg
2½ tablespoons flour
2 tablespoons milk
3 tablespoons grated tasty
   cheddar cheese

salt and pepper
1 medium-sized potato, grated
1 teaspoon Edmonds baking powder
cooking oil for frying

Beat egg; add flour, milk, cheese and seasonings. Add potato and baking powder just before frying. Shallow fry in hot oil 5 minutes on each side. Serve hot. garnished with parsley.

My best-loved recipe was Mock Whitebait Fritters. My mother could make a fritter out of anything, but these were the family favourite. I remember the main ingredients were chopped onion, grated cheese and grated raw potato. They were perfect when they were 'al dente' and to me, as a small child, they surpassed the real whitebait fritters because they did not have those little eyes to stare accusingly as you ate.

ELLIE HENDERSON, MOTUEKA

MEAT

COOKING MEAT

GUIDE TO ROASTING MEAT AT 160°C–180°C

Meat		Minutes per 500 g	Internal Temp °C
Beef	rare	20–30	60–65
	medium	25–35	70–73
	well done	40–45	75–78
Lamb	medium rare	20–30	70–73
	medium	25–30	75–78
	well done	35–40	79–82
Mutton	well done	35–45	79–82
Pork	medium	25–35	71
	well done	40–45	76
Veal	well done	35–40	75–78

APPROXIMATE TIMES FOR GRILLING MEAT

BEEF STEAKS (2–2.5 CM THICK)

rare	3–4 minutes each side
medium	5–6 minutes each side
well done	6 minutes each side, then reduce heat and cook to your liking

LAMB AND MUTTON CHOPS

medium	5–6 minutes each side
well done	7–8 minutes each side

PORK STEAKS AND CHOPS

medium	4–6 minutes each side
well done	7–8 minutes each side

Grilling times depend on the thickness of the meat and its temperature immediately before cooking. All meats should ideally be at room temperature before grilling.

TO SIMMER MEAT

Calculate the cooking time, allowing 30 to 40 minutes per 500 g.

- Fresh meat (mutton, etc). Place meat in a saucepan with sufficient hot water to cover. Bring to the boil. Add 1 teaspoon salt. Cover and simmer gently until the meat is tender. Garnish with vegetables and serve with Parsley Sauce.
- Salt meat (corned beef, etc). Place meat in cold water with a little vinegar, 1 onion and a few pickling spices. Cover. Bring to the boil then simmer gently until the meat is tender. Corned beef is improved by the addition of 1 tablespoon golden syrup (or a little sugar) to the water.

CARVING TIPS

- Leave the roast in a warm place for 10 to 15 minutes before carving. This allows the meat to 'set' and makes it easier to carve.
- Use a really sharp carving knife. Hold the meat with a carving fork.
- Cut across the fibres and the meat will appear to be more tender.

TRADITIONAL MEAT ACCOMPANIMENTS

Roast beef	horseradish sauce, mustard, Yorkshire pudding, brown gravy.
Corned beef	mustard sauce.
Roast lamb	mint sauce or jelly, gravy.
Boiled mutton	caper, onion or parsley sauce.
Roast pork	apple sauce or rings, pineapple, gravy.
Roast veal	sausagemeat stuffing or balls, sausages and bacon rolls, gravy.

GRAVY

1 tablespoon fat in roasting dish
1½ to 3 tablespoons Edmonds standard
   grade flour

1 cup water, liquid stock or vegetable water
salt
pepper

Pour off fat from roasting dish, leaving 1 tablespoon. Sprinkle flour into pan. Use 1½ tablespoons for thin gravy and up to 3 tablespoons for thick gravy. Lightly brown the flour over a medium heat. Add the water slowly, stirring constantly. Stir until boiling. Season with salt and pepper to taste. Pour into a warmed gravy boat or jug.

Steak and Kidney Pie was always good tucker after helping out on the farm.

DAVID MADDOX, WHANGAREI

As a new bride and wanting to impress, Spanish Sausages was the first meal I cooked for my husband in 1965. He was delighted with the result — and today we're still going strong. Five children later, Edmonds cookbook was always there for any occasion.

C. RAE QUIRKE, FEILDING

My favourite recipe is the Braised Lamb Knuckles. I love it because it is so simple and yet absolutely delicious. It's great to cook for two, or for a dinner party — and guests think it's amazing!

SALLY FREWIN, GREY LYNN, AUCKLAND

ABERDEEN SAUSAGE

500 g steak
50 g bacon
500 g sausage meat
1 tablespoon Worcestershire sauce

1 beef stock cube
salt and pepper
1 egg, beaten
225 g breadcrumbs

Mince steak and bacon, add remainder of ingredients. Bind with beaten egg and form into a roll. Put in a floured cloth and boil 1½ hours. Roll in brown, dry breadcrumbs. Serve cold.

BEEF OLIVES   SERVES 4

1 cup soft breadcrumbs
½ cup chopped pitted prunes
1 small onion, finely chopped
½ teaspoon grated lemon rind
½ teaspoon thyme
6 pieces (600 g) beef schnitzel

2 tablespoons cooking oil
2 tablespoons Edmonds standard
    grade flour
1½ cups liquid beef stock
2 tablespoons soy sauce

Combine breadcrumbs, prunes, onion, lemon rind and thyme. Lay pieces of schnitzel out flat. Divide breadcrumb mixture evenly among pieces of meat. Spread each piece of meat with breadcrumb mixture then roll up like a sponge roll. Secure with toothpicks. Heat oil in a frying pan. Add beef olives and brown on all sides. Transfer to a casserole dish. Stir flour into frying pan and cook for 1 minute. Gradually add stock, stirring constantly. Bring to the boil. Add soy sauce. Pour this over beef olives. Cook at 160°C for 45 minutes or until meat is tender. Remove toothpicks before serving.

PORK OLIVES
Use pork schnitzel in place of beef in the above recipe. It may be necessary to double the number of schnitzel as pork pieces are usually smaller in size.

I find it very difficult to decide on which is my favourite Edmonds recipe as there are so many. But I would have to choose the Beef Pot Roast because I cook this for each of my three families when they come to tea. All three sets of parents are busy working and just love to be able to sit down and have a tasty, old-fashioned meal like this lovely dish. The grandchildren also love it and, in this day of fast and convenient foods, it will be nice if they can carry on cooking these lovely old-fashioned, healthy meals.

CAROL WATSON, NORTHCOTE, AUCKLAND

BEEF POT ROAST

1 tablespoon cooking oil
1 kg piece beef topside, trimmed
32 g packet onion soup mix
1 cup liquid beef stock

1 bay leaf
1 tablespoon Edmonds Fielder's cornflour
1 tablespoon water
1 teaspoon wholegrain mustard

Heat the oil in a large saucepan. Add the meat and brown well on all sides. Remove meat from pan and pour off fat. Return meat to pan. In a bowl, combine soup mix and stock. Pour this over the meat. Add bay leaf. Cover, bring to the boil, reduce heat and simmer gently for 3 hours or until meat is tender. Check liquid level from time to time, adding a little water if necessary. Remove bay leaf. In a bowl, combine cornflour and water, mixing until smooth. Remove meat from pan. Add cornflour mixture to the pan. Bring to the boil, stirring constantly until mixture thickens. Add mustard. Serve with sliced meat. If wished, potato and carrot can be added to the pan 30 minutes before end of cooking time.

BEEF STEW

1 kg beef steak
2 tablespoons Edmonds standard
    grade flour
pepper and salt
2 tablespoons cooking oil

2 onions, sliced
water (about 1 cup)
1 carrot, peeled and diced
1 turnip, peeled and diced
4 potatoes, peeled and diced

Remove fat from meat, cut into neat pieces. Season flour with salt and pepper. Roll meat pieces in flour to coat. Heat oil in a saucepan. Brown meat. Remove from pan. Add onions and cook for 3–4 minutes. Return meat to pan. Add water. Simmer for 2 hours. Add diced vegetables 30 minutes before serving. The vegetables are diced to prevent them from going squashy. May be served with dumplings (see page 98).

BEEF STROGANOFF

500 g rump steak
2 tablespoons butter
1 tablespoon cooking oil
1 onion, sliced
150 g mushrooms, sliced

¼ cup white wine
½ cup sour cream
1 tablespoon lemon juice
salt
pepper

Trim fat from meat. Cut meat into thin strips against the grain. Heat butter and oil in a frying pan. Add meat and quickly brown on both sides. Remove from pan and set aside. Add onion and mushrooms to pan. Cook until onion is clear. Return meat to pan. Add wine and sour cream. Reheat gently. Add lemon juice. Season with salt and pepper to taste. Serve with rice.

BRAISED LAMB KNUCKLES

½ cup Edmonds standard grade flour
salt and pepper
8 lamb knuckles, trimmed of excess fat
2 tablespoons cooking oil
1 onion, finely chopped
1 teaspoon crushed garlic
1½ cups red wine

¼ cup tomato puree
2 cups liquid beef stock
1 tablespoon Edmonds Fielder's cornflour
1 tablespoon water
salt and pepper
3 sprigs rosemary

Preheat oven to 150°C. Season flour with salt and pepper. Place in a shallow dish. Roll in the flour mixture to coat. Heat oil in a large, heavy-based frying pan. Cook 4 knuckles at a time, turning occasionally, until browned. Transfer to a roasting pan. Repeat with remaining knuckles. Cover roasting dish and bake at 150°C for 1 hour. Remove dish from oven and pour off excess fat. While knuckles are cooking, add onion to the frying pan and cook for 5 minutes until soft. Add garlic, wine, tomato puree and stock. Mix cornflour to a paste with water. Add to pan, stirring constantly until sauce thickens slightly and comes to the boil. Season. Pour over knuckles. Lay rosemary on top. Cover dish tightly with foil. Bake at 150°C for 2 hours, turning knuckles occasionally. Serve with mashed potato. Garnish with sprigs of rosemary.

CORNED BEEF

1 kg corned silverside
1 bay leaf
sprig parsley
4 black peppercorns

1 tablespoon golden syrup
1 thinly peeled strip orange rind
1 tablespoon malt vinegar

Put silverside in a saucepan. Add bay leaf, parsley, peppercorns, golden syrup, orange rind and vinegar. Barely cover with water. Cover and bring to the boil then simmer gently for 1 hour or until meat is tender. Drain. Serve hot.or cold with Mustard Sauce (see page 115) or Plum Sauce (see page 147).

CURRY AND RICE

500 g mutton or beef, cubed
2 tablespoons Edmonds standard grade flour
2 tablespoons cooking oil
1 onion, chopped
1 apple, peeled and diced

2 teaspoons curry powder
2 teaspoons chutney
1 teaspoon salt
2 beef stock cubes
450 ml boiling water

Roll meat in flour to coat. Heat oil in a saucepan. Cook meat, onion and apple for 4–5 minutes. Add curry powder and seasonings, then add the stock cubes crumbled and dissolved in the boiling water. Bring to simmering point and cook gently for 2 hours. Coconut or raisins may be added. Serve with boiled rice.

CURRIED SAUSAGES

2 teaspoons cooking oil
8 sausages
1 onion, chopped
1 teaspoon hot curry powder

1 tablespoon Edmonds standard
  grade flour
½ cup liquid beef stock
1 tablespoon relish or chutney

Heat oil in a frying pan. Cook sausages for 10 minutes or until golden on all sides and cooked through. Remove sausages from pan and pour off all but 2 tablespoons of fat. And onion and cook until clear. Stir in curry powder and cook for 30 seconds. Stir in flour and cook for 30 seconds. Gradually add stock, stirring constantly until mixture boils. Slice the sausages. Reduce heat and add relish and sausages. Cook for a further 5 minutes to heat through. Slice sausages and serve with rice.

FRENCH STEAK

750 g stewing steak
½ cup Edmonds standard grade flour
1 teaspoon salt
2 teaspoons sugar
⅛ teaspoon ground cloves
⅛ teaspoon pepper

1 beef stock cube
4 onions, sliced
2 carrots, sliced thinly
2 tablespoons malt vinegar
cold water to barely cover

Preheat over to 160°C. Remove fat and sinews from the steak, cut into about eight servings. Place in the bottom of a casserole and knead flour and seasonings into it. Add onions and carrots. Pour vinegar over and barely cover with water. Cook slowly for at least two hours at 160°C.

HAMBURGER STEAKS

500 g lean beef mince
32 g packet onion soup mix
½ cup soft breadcrumbs
¼ cup tomato sauce

black pepper
1 egg, lightly beaten
cooking oil for frying

Put mince into a bowl. Add soup mix, breadcrumbs, tomato sauce, pepper to taste and egg. Mix to combine. Shape mixture into 6 patties. Heat oil in a frying pan and cook patties over a low heat until browned and cooked through. Alternatively brush each meat patty with oil and grill until juices run clear when tested with a skewer.

IRISH STEW

SERVES 4 TO 6

1 kg hogget shoulder chops, fat removed
6 potatoes, sliced
3 onions, sliced
3 carrots, sliced

2 cups liquid beef stock
salt
black pepper
1 tablespoon chopped parsley

Put chops, potatoes, onions, carrots and beef stock into a large saucepan. Cover, bring to the boil. Reduce heat and simmer for 1½ hours or until meat is tender. Season with salt and pepper to taste. Garnish with parsley.

LAMB CURRY

SERVES 4

1½ tablespoons Edmonds standard
   grade flour
salt
pepper
750 g diced lamb
cooking oil
1 large onion, chopped
2 cloves garlic, crushed

1 tablespoon tomato paste
1½ teaspoons grated root ginger
1 teaspoon chopped fresh chilli
1½ teaspoons ground cumin
1 teaspoon ground coriander
1 teaspoon ground cardamom
½ cup liquid chicken stock

Combine flour, salt and pepper in a bowl. Coat meat in seasoned flour. Set aside. Heat oil in a large saucepan. Add onion and garlic and cook until onion is clear. Remove with slotted spoon. Add half of the meat to pan and quickly brown all over. Remove from pan and repeat with remaining meat. Return meat and onion mixture to saucepan. Add tomato paste, ginger, chilli, cumin, coriander, cardamom and stock, stirring well. Bring to the boil. Cover, reduce heat and simmer gently for 1 hour or until meat is tender. Serve with cucumber salad and poppadoms.

ORIENTAL BEEF AND GINGER CASSEROLE

SERVES 4

1 tablespoon pure olive oil
1 clove garlic, crushed
1 onion, sliced
600 g diced braising steak
100 g button mushrooms
2 carrots, sliced

2 tablespoons grated root ginger
1 tablespoon soy sauce
1 tablespoon clear honey
350 ml liquid beef stock
salt and freshly ground
black pepper

Preheat oven to 160°C. Heat oil in a large frying pan. Cook garlic and onion for 2 minutes or until softened. Add beef and brown for 5 minutes. Place onions, garlic and beef in a large casserole dish with mushrooms, carrots, ginger, soy sauce, honey and stock. Season well with salt and pepper. Cover and cook for 1½ to 2 hours.

MEATLOAF

500 g lean beef mince
500 g sausage meat
1 onion, finely chopped
2 cloves garlic, crushed
1 egg
1 cup grated carrot
½ cup chopped parsley
2 teaspoons prepared mustard
2 teaspoons mixed herbs

1 teaspoon salt
black pepper

TOPPING
1¼ cup rolled oats
2 tablespoons brown sugar
¼ cup tomato sauce
¼ cup chopped parsley

Combine mince, sausage meat, onion, garlic, egg, carrot, parsley, mustard and herbs, with salt and pepper to taste. Mix well. Press mixture into a 22 cm loaf tin. Combine all topping ingredients and spread evenly over top of meatloaf. Cover with foil and cook at 190°C for 30 minutes. Remove foil and cook for a further 30 minutes or until juices run clear when tested with a skewer. Serve hot.or cold.

MINCE PIE

1 tablespoon cooking oil
1 onion, finely chopped
2 cloves garlic, crushed
500 g lean beef mince
1½ tablespoons Edmonds standard
   grade flour
½ cup liquid beef stock

2 tablespoons tomato puree
salt
black pepper
400 g FLAKY OR SHORT PASTRY (see page 70)
1 egg yolk
1 tablespoon water

Preheat oven to 200°C. Heat oil in a frying pan. Add onion and garlic and cook until onion is golden, stirring constantly. Add mince and cook quickly until meat is browned and crumbly. Stir in flour and cook for 30 seconds. Gradually add stock. Bring to the boil, stirring constantly. Stir in tomato puree, salt and pepper to taste. Simmer gently for 10 minutes. Set aside to cool. Cut pastry in half. On a lightly floured board roll out one portion and line a 22 cm pie plate. Trim off excess. Wet edge of pastry. Spoon meat filling onto pastry. Roll remaining pastry to fit top of plate. Carefully place pastry over filling. Press edges firmly together. Decorate with any pastry trimmings. Combine egg yolk and water and brush over pastry. Make two holes in the centre of pastry. Bake at 200°C for 25 minutes or until golden.

OXTAIL STEW

1 oxtail
2 tablespoons Edmonds standard
   grade flour
2 tablespoons cooking oil
2 onions, sliced

2 carrots, peeled and sliced
salt and pepper
2 beef stock cubes dissolved in 2 cups
   boiling water

Joint the oxtail, roll each piece in flour. Heat oil in saucepan. Cook oxtail until brown. Lift out meat and add vegetables. Cook until brown. Return oxtail to pan. Add seasonings and just enough of the beef stock liquid to cover the meat and vegetables. Simmer about 3 hours.

QUICK SPAGHETTI BOLOGNESE

500 g minced beef
1 packet oxtail soup
1 stick celery, chopped
½ cup cooked peas
1 cup water

1 beef stock cube
4 mushrooms, sliced
1 medium sized tin spaghetti
½ cup grated tasty cheddar cheese

Place mince, soup, celery and peas in a medium sized saucepan. Add the water into which the stock cube has been crumbled, and bring to the boil. Reduce the heat and simmer for 10 minutes stirring occasionally. Add the mushrooms and spaghetti and cook for a further 5 minutes. Place mixture into a serving dish and sprinkle with grated cheese.

SHEPHERD'S PIE   SERVES 4

1 tablespoon cooking oil
1 onion, chopped
500 g lean beef mince
2 tablespoons Edmonds standard
   grade flour
1 tablespoon tomato sauce
1 tablespoon sweet fruit chutney
¾ cup liquid beef stock

KUMARA TOPPING
4 kumara, peeled and chopped
1 tablespoon butter
1 small onion, finely chopped
½ cup grated tasty cheddar cheese
salt and freshly ground black
   pepper to season

Preheat oven to 190°C. Heat oil in a large frying pan. Add first onion and cook until clear. Add mince and cook until well browned, stirring constantly. Stir in flour and cook for 1 minute. Add tomato sauce, chutney and stock. Bring to the boil, reduce heat and simmer for 5 minutes. Set aside. Cook kumara in boiling, salted water until tender. Drain and heat for a few minutes to dry off excess moisture. Shake pan frequently during this time. Mash kumara. Add butter, second onion and half of the cheese, mixing until smooth and creamy. Season with salt and pepper to taste. Put mince into a pie dish. Top with kumara mixture. Sprinkle with remaining cheese. Bake at 190°C for 20 minutes or until golden and heated through.

PAVLOVA
JELLY CREAMS
ORANGE CAKES

FROM EDMONDS COOKERY BOOK, 4TH DE LUXE EDITION (1959).

● TRIFLE

Sponge (preferably stale), canned or bottled fruit, *Edmonds* Jelly, Sherry or Brandy (optional), *Edmonds* Custard.

Soak sponge in a little of fruit juice with sherry or brandy if used. Place layers of sponge and fruit in a bowl and pour a little cool liquid jelly over the top. Continue layers until the bowl is nearly full, pour custard over top and chill. Garnish with whipped cream and choice fruits.

FROM EDMONDS COOKERY BOOK, 12TH DE LUXE EDITION (1972).

SPAGHETTI AND MEATBALLS

SAUCE
1 tablespoon cooking oil
1 clove garlic, crushed
1 onion, chopped
400 g can tomatoes in juice, puréed
¼ cup tomato paste
salt
pepper

MEATBALLS
500 g lean beef mince
2 tablespoons tomato sauce
1 onion, finely chopped
1 clove garlic, crushed
1 teaspoon curry powder
½ cup soft breadcrumbs
500 g packet spaghetti, cooked

SAUCE: Heat oil in a saucepan. Add garlic and onion. Cook until golden. Add to pan. Bring to the boil. Stir in tomato paste. Reduce heat and simmer for 10 to 15 minutes or until thickened to a sauce consistency. Season. Keep warm until meatballs are ready.

MEATBALLS: Preheat oven to 200°C. Put mince, tomato sauce, onion, garlic, curry powder and breadcrumbs in a bowl. Mix thoroughly. Measure tablespoons of mixture and shape into balls. Place on an oven tray or in a shallow ovenproof dish. Cook at 200°C for 8 to 10 minutes or until cooked through. To serve, add hot meatballs to the prepared sauce and coat. Spoon on top of spaghetti.

STEAK AND KIDNEY PIE

400 g beef chuck or blade steak
100 g beef or lamb kidneys
2 tablespoons cooking oil
1 onion, chopped
2 stalks celery, sliced
1 tablespoon Edmonds standard
    grade flour
1 cup liquid beef stock

¼ cup tomato puree
½ teaspoon mixed herbs
salt
black pepper
200 g FLAKY PASTRY (see page 70)
1 egg yolk
1 tablespoon water

Trim fat from meat and cut into 2 cm cubes. Heat oil in a heavy-based frying pan. Add meat in batches and quickly brown on all sides. Using a slotted spoon, remove meat from pan and set aside. Add onion and celery and cook until onion is clear. Stir in flour and cook for 30 seconds. Gradually add stock, stirring constantly. Bring to the boil. Return meat to pan. Stir in tomato puree and herbs. Cover and cook gently for 1 hour or until meat is tender. Season with salt and pepper to taste. Using a slotted spoon, transfer meat and vegetables to a 20 cm pie plate or dish. Pour ¼ cup of the cooking liquid over the meat. Reserve remaining liquid. Allow to cool. Preheat oven to 200°C. On a lightly floured board roll out pastry to 3 cm larger than the pie plate or dish. Cut a 3 cm wide strip off the edge. Wet edge of pie plate with water and place the pastry strip all round. Cover with pastry round, pressing edges firmly together. Pierce holes in centre of pie. Decorate with any pastry trimmings. Beat egg yolk and water together. Brush over pastry. Bake at 220°C for 20 minutes or until golden and well risen. Reheat reserved cooking liquid and serve with the pie.

SPANISH SAUSAGES

6 pork sausages
6 rashers bacon
1 onion, sliced
1 carrot, peeled and sliced

1 tablespoon tomato sauce
1 teaspoon mixed herbs
salt and pepper
a little water

Preheat oven to 150°C. Wrap sausages in bacon and fry until crisp. Put in a casserole with a little water, sliced vegetables, sauce and seasonings. Cook at 150°C for 1 hour.

DUMPLINGS   SERVES 4 TO 6

1½ cups Edmonds standard grade flour
2 teaspoons Edmonds baking powder
¼ teaspoon salt
½ teaspoon mixed herbs

1 tablespoon finely chopped onion
100 g butter
½ cup milk, approximately

Sift flour, baking powder and salt into a bowl. Stir in herbs and onion. Rub butter into dry ingredients until mixture resembles coarse breadcrumbs. Add enough milk to mix to a soft dough. Drop large spoonsful of dough on top of boiling stew. Cover and cook for 10 minutes or until dumplings are cooked through.

YORKSHIRE PUDDING   SERVES 6

1 cup Edmonds standard grade flour
½ teaspoon salt
2 eggs

½ cup milk
2 tablespoons water
2 tablespoons cooking oil

Sift flour and salt into a bowl. Make a well in the centre. Add eggs. Lightly beat together then gradually add milk and water, mixing to a smooth batter. Chill for 1 hour. Stir again. Preheat oven to 200°C. Heat oil in a roasting dish until smoking hot. Quickly pour batter into roasting dish. Bake at 200°C for 30 minutes or until golden, well risen and crisp around the edges. Cut into squares and serve with roast beef.

As a teenager leaving home and having to cook for myself for the very first time, my efforts were directed towards meals I'd been used to at home. For years the norm had been meat and veg every Sunday with the remains recycled in the early part of the week. Roast beef always featured prominently and, as both my parents were from Yorkshire, Yorkshire Pudding was nearly always an accompaniment. Cooking roast beef and vegetables did not seem too much of a difficulty, but the Yorkshire Pud required a bit more effort. After most early attempts were reasonably successful, I ventured into other areas of the cookery book, but the Yorkshire Pudding was always a favourite and has remained so.

ALWYN PALMER, BELMONT, LOWER HUTT

POULTRY

ROAST CHICKEN

As soon as chicken is sufficiently thawed, remove giblets (if present) from body cavity. Simmer them in water with seasoning (e.g. a small onion, peppercorns, bay leaf and parsley) to provide a stock for gravy. When chicken is fully thawed, wash and dry it inside and out. Sprinkle body cavity with salt.

Unstuffed: Place in body cavity a large knob of butter, fresh herbs and a lemon wedge or clove of garlic.
Stuffed: Pack cavity loosely with stuffing of your choice. Close body openings (sew, skewer or pin with clean safety pins). Truss the chicken, with wings folded under body and legs tied together. Weigh the stuffed bird.
Roasting: Preheat oven to 180°C. Place chicken in roasting pan (or oven bag). Brush skin with melted butter (or lemon juice) and sprinkle with salt and pepper to taste. Roast, allowing approximately 55 minutes per kilogram or stuffed weight, plus 20 minutes.

A CHICKEN IN AN OVEN BAG TAKES APPROXIMATELY 40 MINUTES PER KILOGRAM.

Baste during cooking. A larger size chicken should be turned once or twice.

The oven temperature can be raised to 200°C for the last 10 to 15 minutes to allow the chicken to crisp. The chicken is cooked when a skewer inserted in the thickest part of the thigh shows a colourless liquid, with no trace of pink, and the joints can be moved easily.

Turn off oven and remove cooked chicken from roasting pan (or oven bag). Place on carving dish and return to oven 5 to 10 minutes. This allows the juices to be absorbed for full flavour and ease of carving.

STUFFINGS

Basic Bread Stuffing
1 large onion
75 g butter
12 slices of bread

salt and pepper
1 teaspoon sage
2 eggs, beaten (optional) or water

Chop the onion and cook in butter till tender. Cube the bread and combine with the onion and butter, and seasoning. Add the beaten eggs or sufficient water to moisten the stuffing. The giblets (if present) can be simmered in salted water till tender, chopped and added to the stuffing.

Mushroom Stuffing: Add 100 g of sliced mushrooms to the onion. Toss with the bread stuffing.
Orange Stuffing: Replace one egg or part of the liquid with orange juice. Add the finely slivered rind of an orange.
Apricot Stuffing: Add half a cup of finely sliced dried apricots.
Celery Stuffing: Add half a cup of finely sliced celery when cooking the onion.

FRUIT STUFFING: Add a grated apple, half a cup of crushed pineapple and 50 g raisins. Omit eggs.

BANANA STUFFING: Add one cup ripe diced banana.

WALNUT STUFFING: Add 75 g chopped walnuts and one tablespoon Worcestershire sauce to celery stuffing above.

My favourite recipe is the Roast Chicken with sage stuffing. When I was about eighteen years old, I thought I'd be brave and give it a go. Now I have about fifty cookbooks and love cooking.
CORIN BICKERTON, BLENHEIM

APRICOT CHICKEN

SERVES 4 TO 6

6 chicken pieces
cooking oil for frying

SAUCE
425 g can apricot halves with juice
½ teaspoon grated lemon or lime rind
2 tablespoons lemon or lime juice

½ teaspoon ground ginger
2 tablespoons Edmonds Fielder's cornflour
1 tablespoon spiced vinegar
½ teaspoon sugar
salt
pepper

Remove skin and fat from chicken pieces. Heat oil in a frying pan and cook chicken for 10 minutes each side or until juices run clear when tested. Drain on absorbent paper. Pour apricot sauce over chicken.

SAUCE: Purée apricots and juice in a food processor or blender. Put purée in a saucepan. Add lemon rind, juice, ginger and cornflour. Mix well. Gently heat, stirring constantly until mixture boils and thickens. Stir in vinegar, sugar, salt and pepper to taste.

CHICKEN AND ORANGE CASSEROLE

SERVES 4 TO 6

1 kg chicken pieces
1 tablespoon butter
1 onion, finely chopped
1 cup sliced celery
½ cup orange juice
½ cup liquid chicken stock

¼ teaspoon cinnamon
⅛ teaspoon ground allspice
1 tablespoon grated orange rind
1 tablespoon Edmonds Fielder's cornflour
1 tablespoon white vinegar
orange slices

Preheat oven to 180°C. Remove skin and fat from chicken. Melt butter in a large frying pan or flameproof casserole dish. Add chicken and quickly brown on all sides. Remove from pan and set aside. Add onion and celery. Cook until onion is clear. Add orange juice, stock, cinnamon, allspice and orange rind. Bring to the boil. Add chicken. Cover and bake at 180°C for 40 minutes or until juices run clear when tested. Alternatively, to continue cooking on top of stove, reduce heat, cover and simmer gently for 30 minutes. Mix cornflour and vinegar to a smooth paste. Add to chicken mixture. Stir until mixture thickens. Garnish with orange slices.

CHICKEN AND PESTO BAKE

SERVES 4 TO 6

8 chicken drumsticks
¼ cup Pesto (see below)
¾ cup toasted breadcrumbs
sprigs of fresh basil to garnish

PESTO
1 tablespoon canola oil
2 tablespoons pinenuts
3 cloves garlic, chopped
2 cups fresh basil leaves
¼ cup canola oil
salt and pepper to season

Preheat oven to 190°C. Remove skin from chicken. Brush or spread drumsticks with pesto. Coat with breadcrumbs. Place in a greased roasting dish and bake at 190°C for 35 minutes or until juices run clear when tested. Garnish with sprigs of fresh basil.

PESTO: Heat first measure of oil in a small frying pan. Add pinenuts and cook, stirring frequently, until golden. Drain on absorbent paper. Put the garlic, basil and pine nuts into the bowl of a food processor or blender. Process until finely chopped. Continue processing while adding second measure of oil in a thin, steady stream. Process for a few seconds until just combined. Season with salt and pepper to taste. Makes about ½ cup.

CHICKEN CREOLE

SERVES 4 TO 6

medium sized chicken
2 onions, chopped
1 green pepper, chopped
1 ham steak, chopped
140 g pot tomato paste

400 g can tomatoes in juice, chopped
¼ teaspoon chopped basil
50 g salami, chopped
salt
black pepper

Preheat oven to 180°C. Remove neck and giblets from chicken, if present. Place chicken in a large ovenproof dish. Add onions, green pepper, ham steak, tomato paste, tomatoes and juice. Cover and cook at 180°C for 1½ hours or until juices run clear when tested. Add basil and salami. Stir in salt and pepper to taste. Serve with rice.

CHICKEN CURRY

SERVES 4

1 tablespoon cooking oil
2 cloves garlic, crushed
1 onion, chopped
1 teaspoon grated root ginger

1 tablespoon curry powder
1 cup liquid chicken stock
4 chicken breasts

Heat oil in a large frying pan. Add garlic, onion and ginger. Cook until onion is clear. Stir in curry powder and cook for 30 seconds. Add stock and chicken. Cover and bring to the boil. Reduce heat and simmer for 30 minutes or until chicken is tender. Serve with rice.

COQ AU VIN

25 g butter
2 rashers bacon, chopped
8 pieces chicken
12 pickling onions, peeled
100 g button mushrooms
2 tablespoons brandy
1½ cups red wine
2 cloves garlic, crushed
1 tablespoon tomato paste

1 bay leaf
sprig thyme
sprig parsley
salt
pepper
2 tablespoons Edmonds standard
    grade flour
25 g butter

Melt first measure of butter in a flameproof casserole dish or saucepan. Add bacon and cook for 4 minutes. Remove from pan. Remove skin from chicken. Add chicken to pan and cook until browned on both sides. Remove from pan. Add onions and cook until golden. Return bacon and chicken to pan. Add mushrooms. Pour brandy over chicken. Stir in wine, garlic and tomato paste. Make a bouquet garni with bay leaf, thyme and parsley. Add to saucepan. Bring to the boil. Cover, reduce heat and simmer gently for 45 minutes or until chicken is tender. Season with salt and pepper to taste. Put flour and second measure of butter into a small bowl. Mix together to form a paste called beurre manié. Remove chicken from pan and keep warm. Bring cooking liquid to the boil and whisk in the beurre manié a little at a time, cooking gently until sauce is smooth and thickened slightly. Remove bouquet garni. Return chicken to the pan and serve.

CRUNCHY-COATED CHICKEN

3 cups cornflakes, crushed
½ cup coconut
2 tablespoons grated orange rind
2 teaspoons chicken stock powder
1 teaspoon ground nutmeg
1 teaspoon ground ginger

¼ cup Edmonds standard grade flour,
    approximately
½ teaspoon salt
black pepper
1 egg
2 tablespoons water
1 kg chicken pieces

Preheat oven to 180°C. Combine cornflakes, coconut, orange rind, stock powder, nutmeg and ginger. Remove skin and fat from chicken. Combine flour, salt and pepper to taste. Coat chicken with seasoned flour. Lightly beat egg and water together. Dip chicken pieces into egg mixture. Coat in cornflake mixture. Place chicken on a rack in roasting dish. Cook at 180°C for 40 minutes or until juices run clear when tested.

FAMILY CHICKEN PIE

8 boneless chicken thighs
2 tablespoons cooking oil
3 rashers bacon, chopped
100 g mushrooms
1 onion, chopped
1 clove garlic, crushed
2 tablespoons Edmonds standard
    grade flour

1 cup liquid chicken stock
¼ teaspoon mixed herbs
½ cup milk
½ teaspoon salt
white pepper
1 cup drained canned corn kernels
200 g Flaky Pastry (see page 70)
1 egg yolk

Remove skin from chicken. Cut flesh into 2.5 cm cubes. Heat oil in a large saucepan. Add bacon, mushrooms, onion and garlic. Cook until onion is clear. Stir in flour and cook until frothy. Gradually add stock and bring to the boil. Add chicken, herbs, milk, salt and pepper to taste. Reduce heat and cook gently for 20 minutes or until juices run clear when tested, stirring occasionally. Remove from heat and allow to cool. Stir in corn. Preheat oven to 220°C. Pour chicken mixture into a 20 cm pie dish. Brush edge of dish with water. On a lightly floured board roll out pastry to a circle large enough to fit top of pie dish. Carefully place pastry over filling. Press edges firmly to seal, then trim. Decorate pie with pastry trimmings. Cut steam holes in centre of pastry top. Brush pastry with egg yolk. Bake at 220°C for 20 minutes or until pastry is golden and well risen.

MOCK CHICKEN

1 onion, medium
butter
1 tomato, skinned and sliced
1 teaspoon mixed herbs

salt
pepper
1 egg, beaten
parsley, to ganish

Chop onion finely and cook in a little butter, but do not brown. Add a tomato, mixed herbs, salt and pepper and egg. Cook slowly until mixture thickens. Pile on cheese or water biscuits and garnish with parsley.

MOCK CHICKEN CONTAINS NO CHICKEN AT ALL. DUE TO SHORTAGES OR RATIONING OF FOODS IN THE DEPRESSION AND WORLD WAR ERAS, WOMEN HAD TO BE CREATIVE IN COOKING FOR THEIR FAMILIES. MANY 'MOCK' RECIPES WERE INVENTED IN THESE TIMES AND SOME, LIKE MOCK CHICKEN, SURVIVE TODAY.

SALADS & VEGETABLES

COLESLAW

1 small cabbage, finely shredded
½ green pepper, sliced finely
½ red pepper, sliced finely
1 to 2 sticks diced celery
1 tablespoon finely chopped onion

1 carrot, peeled and grated
½ teaspoon salt
½ teaspoon paprika

FRENCH DRESSING (see page 114)

Mix cabbage with peppers, celery, onion, carrot, salt and paprika. Chill thoroughly for 2 hours. Just before serving mix with chilled dressing and toss well together.

EGG SALAD

3 courgettes, thinly sliced
¼ cup chopped parsley
6 hard-boiled eggs

¾ cup MAYONNAISE (see page 114)
1 clove garlic, crushed
salt, black pepper

Combine courgettes and parsley in a bowl. Shell and chop the eggs. Add to courgettes. Combine Mayonnaise and garlic. Season to taste with salt and pepper. Pour dressing over salad. Stir to combine. Chill before serving.

LUNCHBOX PASTA SALAD

150 g dried pasta bows
12 cherry tomatoes, halved (or 4 tomatoes, quartered)
1 green capsicum, seeded, cored and diced
100 g cheddar cheese, cut in small dice
½ cup toasted pinenuts (optional)

DRESSING
2 tablespoons extra virgin olive oil
2 tablespoons white wine vinegar
2 tablespoons freshly squeezed orange juice
1 tablespoon chopped parsley
salt and freshly ground black pepper to season

Cook pasta according to packet instructions. Transfer to a sieve. Cool under cold running water, then drain thoroughly. Combine all salad ingredients in a large bowl. Pour over dressing and toss to combine. To make the dressing, place all ingredients in a jar. Secure the lid and shake vigorously. To include this salad in the lunch box, transfer to a lidded container.

POTATO SALAD

SERVES 4 TO 6

2 to 3 cups diced cooked potato
2 to 3 spring onions, sliced
2 hard-boiled eggs, chopped

1 to 2 teaspoons finely chopped mint
½ to 1 cup MAYONNAISE (see page 114)

Gently combine all ingredients. Chill before serving.

VARIATIONS
Any of the following can be added:
1 green or red pepper, sliced
1 tablespoon chopped chives or parsley
2 to 3 rashers bacon, cooked and diced

¼ cup toasted sunflower or sesame seeds
¼ cup sliced gherkins
4 radishes, sliced

RICE SALAD

SERVES 6 TO 8

1 cup long grain rice
½ cup raisins or sultanas
1 green or red pepper, sliced

½ to 1 cup pineapple pieces
¼ cup FRENCH DRESSING (see page 114)

Cook rice according to packet directions. Drain and cool. Add raisins, pepper and pineapple to rice. Pour dressing over rice. Toss to combine. Chill before serving.

WALDORF SALAD

2 to 3 apples, cut in chunks with
    skin on
2 to 3 oranges, peeled and
    cut in chunks
1 to 2 cups diced celery

½ cup walnut pieces
1 cup dressing (use mayonnaise, blue
    cheese, ½ mayonnaise and ½ natural
    yoghurt, cream or sour cream)

Combine ingredients. Pour over dressing and chill. Serve in a bowl or in individual lettuce cups.

VARIATIONS
Add any of the following:
½ cup raisins or chopped dates
Use peanuts or cashew nuts in place
    of walnuts

½ to 1 cup pineapple pieces
¾ cup cubes of cheese
1 to 2 bananas, sliced
½ to 1 cup grapes

METHODS OF COOKING VEGETABLES

BOILING
Put prepared vegetables in a small amount of boiling water. Choose a saucepan large enough to fit vegetables easily. Root vegetables require more cooking water. Cover tightly and bring the water quickly back to boiling point. Cook vegetables over a moderate heat until tender yet firm when tested. Drain well. Serve immediately. Use the cooking water for sauces, soups, or gravy.

STEAMING
Put prepared vegetables in a steamer over rapidly boiling water. Cover tightly and adjust heat to ensure a steady flow of steam. Steam vegetables until just tender. If a steamer is unavailable, place vegetables into a metal sieve. Place sieve over a saucepan of boiling water. Add more boiling water to the steamer or saucepan if necessary. Cover with aluminium foil to keep in the steam. Steam vegetables until just tender. Take care when removing the foil. Serve immediately.

MICROWAVING
Cut vegetables to a similar size. Place in a shallow microwave dish with a small amount of water and cover. If no lid is available, cover with microwave-safe plastic film. Stir once during cooking time. After cooking, leave covered while standing. Standing time is about one-third of total cooking time. Always undercook as cooking continues while standing. Add salt and other seasonings after cooking.

ROASTING
Place oil in a roasting pan and heat in a hot oven. Dry pieces of prepared vegetables. Potato and kumara may be rolled in flour to give a crisp coating. Arrange vegetables around meat or place in roasting pan containing hot oil. Turn vegetables so they are well coated in oil. Roast in moderate oven. Turn vegetables halfway through cooking time. Cook until tender. Remove from roasting dish. Drain on absorbent paper and keep warm until ready to serve.

STIR-FRYING
Suitable vegetables are onion, carrot, mushrooms and all green vegetables. Cut vegetables into bite-sized pieces. A variety of shapes like sticks and rounds makes a stir-fry more interesting. A vegetable may be stir-fried by itself or any combination may be cooked together. Heat a small amount of oil in a frying pan or wok. Add vegetables that require longer cooking first, e.g. broccoli, carrot, cauliflower, onion. Stir occasionally. Partially cook then add remaining vegetables which require shorter cooking. Cook until tender but crisp.

HINTS FOR VEGETABLES
- Choose a variety of vegetables each week for interesting meals and good nutrition.
- Wash vegetables before cutting to remove loose soil and pests.
- Remove any green from potatoes before cooking as this is poisonous.

- Cook beetroot whole, leaving 2 to 3 cm of beetroot tops on the beet to prevent loss of colour during cooking. Cut after cooking.
- If vegetables are to be peeled, pare thinly as precious vitamins and minerals are next to the skin. Soaking prepared vegetables in water leaches out valuable nutrients. Use as little water as possible when cooking vegetables to retain the nutrients.
- Overcooking vegetables destroys valuable nutrients. Cook for as short a time as possible.
- Cover vegetables when boiling or steaming to ensure quick cooking.
- Store fresh vegetables in the refrigerator crisper.
- Store potatoes, onions and pumpkins in a cool, dark, dry place.

CAULIFLOWER CHEESE SERVES 4 TO 6

1 cauliflower, whole
25 g butter
2 tablespoons Edmonds standard grade flour
2 cups milk

½ cup grated tasty cheddar cheese
salt
white pepper
½ teaspoon dry mustard

Preheat oven to 190°C. Cook cauliflower in boiling salted water until tender. While cauliflower is cooking, melt the butter in a saucepan. Stir in flour and cook until frothy. Gradually add milk, stirring constantly until mixture boils and thickens. Remove from heat. Add ¼ cup of the cheese, salt and pepper to taste, and mustard. Drain cauliflower and transfer to an ovenproof serving dish. Pour sauce over the cauliflower. Sprinkle with remaining cheese. Cook at 190°C for 20 minutes or until golden.

CURRIED VEGETABLES

50 g butter
1 onion, sliced
2 potatoes, diced
2 to 3 teaspoons curry powder
1 tablespoon lemon juice
1 tablespoon Edmonds standard
  grade flour

salt and pepper
1 cup water
3 to 4 cups of mixture of chopped or sliced
  raw vegetables such as carrots, beans,
  green pepper, courgettes, mushrooms,
  celery, broccoli and cauliflower

Melt butter in large saucepan and cook onion and potato gently for 5 minutes. Add curry powder, lemon juice, flour, salt and pepper and cook 1 minute. Add water and remaining vegetables. Cover and simmer gently for 5 to 8 minutes or until vegetables are tender. Serve with rice.

MICROWAVE
Reduce water to ½ cup. Place butter in large dish and microwave 30 seconds. Add onion and potato and microwave 1 minute. Add curry powder, lemon juice, flour, salt and pepper and microwave 1 minute. Add water and remaining vegetables. Cover and microwave 6 minutes. Stir after 3 minutes.

RATATOUILLE

¼ cup pure olive oil
6 medium tomatoes, blanched and
  chopped
½ teaspoon salt
black pepper
¼ teaspoon sugar

1 large onion, sliced
2 cloves garlic, crushed
1 green pepper, sliced
250 g courgettes, sliced
1 eggplant, chopped

Heat half the oil in a small saucepan. Add tomatoes, salt, pepper to taste, and sugar.
Cook for 10 minutes or until sauce consistency, stirring frequently. Heat remaining oil
in a large frying pan or saucepan. Add onion and garlic and cook until onion is clear.
Stir in green pepper, courgettes and eggplant. Cover and cook slowly until vegetables
are tender, stirring frequently. Add tomato mixture to the vegetables. Stir to combine.
Serve hot.

SCALLOPED POTATOES

4 medium potatoes, thinly sliced
1 small onion, finely sliced
1 cup grated tasty cheddar cheese

salt
white pepper
1 cup milk

Preheat oven to 180°C. Place a layer of potatoes in a 20 cm diameter casserole dish.
Sprinkle with some onion, cheese, salt and pepper to taste. Repeat until ingredients
are used, ending with a cheese layer. Pour milk over potato mixture. Cover and
cook at 180°C for 30 minutes. Remove lid and continue cooking for a further 10 to 15
minutes or until potatoes are cooked.

STUFFED BAKED POTATOES

4 medium potatoes
2 tablespoons cooking oil
½ cup milk
2 tablespoons butter
salt

black pepper
2 tablespoons chopped parsley
½ cup tasty grated cheese
½ teaspoon paprika

Preheat oven to 180°C. Scrub potatoes and brush with oil. Bake at 180°C for 1 to 1¼
hours or until soft. Cut a lengthwise slice from the top of each potato. Scoop out
potato without breaking skins. Mash potato, milk, butter, salt and pepper to taste, and
parsley. Spoon mixture into potato skins. Sprinkle with cheese and paprika. Bake at
180°C for 5 to 10 minutes or until hot and cheese has melted.

SWEETCORN FRITTERS

SERVES 4 TO 6

¾ cup Edmonds standard grade flour
1 teaspoon Edmonds baking powder
½ teaspoon salt
black pepper

1 egg
440 g can cream-style corn
2 tablespoons cooking oil

Sift flour, baking powder, salt and pepper to taste, into a bowl. Add egg, mixing to combine. Stir in corn. Heat oil in a frying pan. Drop tablespoons of corn mixture into pan. Cook until golden then turn and cook other side. Drain on absorbent paper. Serve hot.

My favourite recipe from my Edmonds cookbook (I used it last night) is Sweetcorn Fritters. This recipe, whatever time of year I make it, always reminds me of summer for some reason. The light and easy recipe is well suited to my style in summer: if it's not relaxed and easy it doesn't get cooked! Very nice with some sweet chilli sauce.

KERRY BORKIN, LINCOLN

Lovely Sweetcorn Fritters always take me back to my childhood summer beach BBQs when we went camping.

TREVOR BUNYAN, PAPAKURA, AUCKLAND

TOMATO FRITTERS

250 g tomatoes
1 cup Edmonds standard grade flour
1 or 2 eggs

¼ teaspoon salt
¼ cup milk
cooking oil to cook

Prick tomatoes with a sharp knife. Place in a bowl. Cover with boiling water for 30 seconds, then drain. Peel skins off tomatoes, discard. Chop tomatoes. Mix all together with yolks of eggs, whisk whites, fold in and fry in hot oil.

The recipe for Tomato Fritters is in an old Edmonds book published in 1952. We have enjoyed them as a lunch dish over the years when tomatoes are plentiful.

LORRAINE TOHILL, OAMARU

VEGETABLE STIR-FRY

2 tablespoons pure olive oil
1 tablespoon finely chopped
   fresh ginger
2 cloves garlic, crushed
2 small onions, quartered and separated
250 g broccoli, cut into florets
¼ cauliflower, cut into florets

1 small bunch spinach, washed, stems
   removed
230 g can bamboo shoots, drained
230 g can water chestnuts, drained
½ cup baby corn
½ cup liquid chicken stock, boiling
2 to 3 spring onions, sliced

Heat oil in a large frying pan or wok. Add ginger, garlic and onions. Stir to coat with oil. Cook for 1 minute. Add remaining vegetables and toss to combine. Stir in stock. Bring to the boil. Cover and cook for 3 minutes or until vegetables are just tender, stirring occasionally. Garnish with spring onions.

VEGETARIAN LASAGNE

25 g butter
1 onion, chopped
2 cloves garlic, crushed
1 small leek, sliced
2 stalks celery, sliced
2 carrots, sliced
2 courgettes, sliced
2 tablespoons Edmonds standard
   grade flour

1 bunch spinach
milk
½ cup grated tasty cheddar cheese
salt
pepper
250 g packet lasagne sheets, cooked
200 g pot natural unsweetened yoghurt
2 eggs
1 cup grated tasty cheddar cheese

Preheat oven to 180°C. Melt butter in a large saucepan. Add onion, garlic and leek. Cook until onion is clear. Add celery, carrots and courgettes. Cover and cook without allowing to colour until celery and carrot are just tender. Add flour and cook until frothy. Remove from heat. Wash spinach thoroughly and, with only the water clinging to the leaves, cook until tender. Drain, reserving all the liquid. Measure liquid and make up to 1 cup with milk. Return flour and vegetables to the heat, gradually add the liquid, stirring constantly until mixture boils and thickens. Remove from heat. Add first measure of cheese. Season with salt and pepper to taste. Set aside. Place one-third of lasagne sheets at the bottom of a greased ovenproof dish. Spread with half the vegetable mixture. Repeat layers, finishing with a layer of lasagne. In a bowl lightly beat yoghurt and eggs until combined. Spread this on top of lasagne. Sprinkle second measure of cheese on top. Cook at 180°C for 20 minutes or until golden and heated through.

STEAMED RAINBOW PUDDING •

3 ozs. Butter
3 ozs. Sugar
1 teaspoon Vanilla Essence
2 Eggs
¼ breakfastcup Milk

6 ozs. Flour
1 moderate teaspoon
    Edmonds Baking Powder
Pinch of Salt
1 teaspoon (heaped) Cocoa
Few drops of Cochineal

Cream butter, sugar and vanilla essence together. Beat the eggs and
add alternately with the sifted flour and baking powder. Add milk with
last of the eggs. Divide the mixture into 3 equal portions. Leave one
white, add the cocoa to the second, and the cochineal to the third.
Grease a basin and drop in spoonfuls of different coloured mixtures so
the pudding will have a marbled effect when cut. Cover with buttered
paper and steam 2 hours.
Serve with *Edmonds* Custard.

FROM EDMONDS COOKERY BOOK, 4TH DE LUXE EDITION (1959).

EXCELLENT RECIPES

CHRISTMAS CAKE
CHRISTMAS PLUM PUDDING

FROM EDMONDS COOKERY BOOK, 6TH EDITION.

DRESSINGS & SAUCES

FRENCH DRESSING (VINAIGRETTE)

MAKES 1 CUP

¾ cup canola oil
¼ cup white or cider vinegar or lemon juice
¼ teaspoon dry mustard
salt

black pepper
1 clove garlic, crushed
1 tablespoon chopped parsley, chives or
    fresh basil

Put all ingredients into a screw-top jar. Shake well to combine.

MAYONNAISE

MAKES ABOUT 1 CUP

1 egg yolk
½ teaspoon salt
¼ teaspoon dry mustard

pinch cayenne pepper
1 tablespoon malt vinegar or lemon juice
1 cup canola oil

Mix egg yolk, salt, mustard and cayenne pepper in a bowl. Add vinegar. Very gradually add oil, beating constantly with a whisk or beater. As mixture begins to combine add remaining oil in a fine stream while beating. If mixture is too thick, add more vinegar.

UNCOOKED (CONDENSED MILK) SALAD DRESSING

MAKES ABOUT 2 CUPS

397 g can sweetened condensed milk
1 cup malt vinegar

1 teaspoon salt
2 teaspoons dry mustard

Stir all ingredients until combined. Leave to stand for a few minutes to thicken before using.

The one recipe which has been used by three different generations of our family would be the Uncooked (Condensed Milk) Salad Dressing. Now I know this is a simple recipe but when I make a potato salad I use this salad dressing and everyone raves about it and wants the recipe for it! It has been passed down from my nana to my mother to me and I will do the same when my daughter is old enough to cook.

RACHEL CLARK, MAIREHAU, CHRISTCHURCH

APPLE SAUCE

3 to 4 large cooking apples, peeled and
   chopped
1 tablespoon water

1 tablespoon butter
2 cloves or few drops lemon juice
sugar

Put apples, water, butter and cloves into a saucepan. Simmer until apples are pulped.
Blend or beat with a fork until smooth. Add sugar to taste.

HOLLANDAISE SAUCE

50 g butter
1 tablespoon lemon juice
2 egg yolks

¼ cup cream
½ teaspoon dry mustard
¼ teaspoon salt

Melt the butter in a double boiler. Add lemon juice, egg yolks and cream. Cook, stirring
constantly, until thick and smooth. Do not boil or sauce will curdle. Remove from
heat. Add mustard and salt and beat until smooth.

TOP 20 MUSTARD SAUCE

1 egg
2 tablespoons sugar
1 tablespoon Edmonds standard
   grade flour
2 teaspoons dry mustard

1 cup water or cooking liquid
   from corned beef
¼ cup malt vinegar
salt
pepper

Beat egg and sugar together. Put into a saucepan. Add flour and mustard. Stir in water
and vinegar gradually. Cook over a low heat until mixture thickens. Season with salt
and pepper to taste, adding more sugar if necessary.

RECIPES FOR THIS TYPE OF MUSTARD SAUCE APPEAR IN PUBLICATIONS IN THE 17TH
CENTURY. IT WAS OFTEN USED WITH GAME DISHES (ESPECIALLY RABBIT) BY THE
LOWER CLASSES AND BY THE UPPER CLASSES AS AN ACCOMPANIMENT TO ROAST BEEF
OR CORNED BEEF AT SUNDAY DINNER.

*Mustard Sauce is my favourite Edmonds cookbook recipe — from my Grandma's 1976 recipe
book which I now have. Delicious every single time!*

KENDALL, WELLINGTON

TARTARE SAUCE

1 cup Mayonnaise (see page 114)
1 tablespoon finely chopped capers
  or gherkins

1 tablespoon chopped parsley
1 tablespoon finely chopped onion

Combine all ingredients.

WHITE SAUCE

2 tablespoons butter
2 tablespoons Edmonds standard
  grade flour

1 cup milk
salt and freshly ground black pepper

Melt butter in a small saucepan. Add flour and stir constantly for 2 minutes. Remove from heat. Gradually add milk, stirring constantly. Return pan to the heat, stirring continuously until sauce thickens and comes to the boil. Season to taste with salt and pepper.

My favourite Edmonds recipe has to be the White Sauce. The first time I made it my wife was cooking silverside to welcome my visiting mother. As I recall, as a youngster White Sauce was an integral and essential adornment to the serving. So I was given the task of producing the sauce. In desperation I reached for the Edmonds cookbook and of course, there it was — White Sauce. It was the talk around the meal table, as to how nice the sauce was, so thank you Edmonds, my White Sauces are now my claim to fame!

ROSS SMITH, MANUREWA, AUCKLAND

WORCESTERSHIRE SAUCE

3 onions, chopped
1 kg brown sugar
2 tablespoons ground ginger
4 tablespoons salt
1 orange, sliced roughly

4.5 litres malt vinegar
1.3 kg apples, chopped
½ teaspoon cayenne pepper
2 tablespoons cloves

Put all ingredients into a preserving pan. Boil slowly 3 hours. Strain and bottle. Cork when cold.

COLD DESSERTS

My memory is of the small brownie-coloured early edition Edmonds Cookery Book. There is a coloured inset of jelly recipes which was one of my favourite 'story books'. After World War Two we didn't have many story/picture books and I remember gazing at those few pages and just wishing that maybe Mum would make some of them. She never did; maybe there weren't many jellies around then either.

NITA SMALL, ASHBURTON

As a non milk drinker, eating Ice-Cream Pudding was the only way I managed to take milk when I was pregnant with our two sons in the early 1970s. I continued to cook it during their youth (and since) and it was a great favourite for birthday parties as well. A cheap pudding to make was very important as we were very poor in those days. The Edmonds recipe book was such a good book — the only cookery book essential for a young bride. Thanks so much Edmonds!

GLYNIS POAD, TAURANGA

In 1965 my mother made Ice-Cream Pudding by the bucket load for a friend who had oesophageal cancer as it was the only food she could digest. Of interest; the friend only recently died, outliving the Ice-Cream Pudding maker by twenty years — what a recipe! Continuing the tradition I have made this for two friends having rigorous chemotherapy. I hope the tradition of the pudding eater outliving the maker does not continue!

JEAN O'BOYLE, ROTORUA

My favourite recipe is Meringues in the Revised Centennial Edition of the Edmonds Cookery Book. Diane Harris' Meringues are world famous in Oamaru!

DIANE HARRIS, OAMARU

Growing up in the sixties and seventies having pudding (winter) or dessert (summer) with the evening meal was without question. Spanish Cream and Pineapple Snow are two summer desserts that I remember very clearly and loved, especially Pineapple Snow. Mum would serve these with preserved fruit or Watties Fruit Salad. I should make them for my children I guess!

FELICITY MURRAY, EASTERN BEACH, AUCKLAND

My new favourite recipe (or at least the one my husband loves) is Spanish Cream. I am English and had never heard of it. I saw it in the recipe book and thought 'that's easy, I'll make it for pud'. My husband went into raptures. 'Just like mum used to make when I was a boy.' (He will be fifty this year!)

JULIE HERBERT, ALBANY, AUCKLAND

We went to Nana's every Sunday lunch and regardless of the roast meal served (generally lamb in those days) we had Spanish Cream with preserved fruit for dessert.

JACQUIE MCNAB, WHAKATANE

CAPTAIN AND SHIP

Perfect for a child's party! Set lime jelly in flat glass dishes, one for each person. Cut the ship from a quarter orange or grapefruit rind, well stripped inside. Place in the jelly before quite set. Fill ship with a cargo of chopped nuts, banana cut small, bits of sponge cake, raspberry jam, and cover well with Edmonds Vanilla Custard poured over when cool, and top with dabs of whipped cream. Use a cocktail stick for the mast, with a sail and flag cut from cellophane. Make the captain by spiking two cherries together with a piece of cocktail stick, using them also for legs and arms, and put a green fruit jube telescope under his arm and a piece of almond stuck on for a peak cap.

CHEESECAKE   SERVES 6

250 g packet Digestive biscuits
1 teaspoon grated lemon rind
1 tablespoon lemon juice
75 g butter, melted

FILLING
2 teaspoons gelatine

2 tablespoons water
250 g pot cream cheese
250 g pot sour cream
½ cup sugar
2 tablespoons lemon juice
1 teaspoon lemon rind
1 teaspoon vanilla essence

Finely crush biscuits. Combine biscuit crumbs, lemon rind, juice and butter. Line the base and sides of a 20 cm spring-form tin with biscuit mixture. Chill while preparing filling. Pour filling into prepared base. Chill until set.

FILLING: Combine gelatine and water. Leave to swell for 10 minutes. Beat cream cheese until soft. Add sour cream and beat until well combined. Add sugar, lemon juice, rind and vanilla. Beat until sugar has dissolved. Dissolve gelatine over hot water. Add to cheese mixture.

EASY CHOCOLATE MOUSSE   SERVES 4 TO 6

150 g cooking chocolate
4 eggs, separated
300 ml cream

2 tablespoons sugar
cream
grated chocolate

Break chocolate into the top of a double boiler. Stir over hot water until chocolate has melted. Allow to cool slightly. Stir yolks into chocolate. Beat until thick and smooth. Beat cream until thick. Quickly fold chocolate mixture into cream. Beat egg whites until stiff but not dry. Gradually add sugar, beating until thick and glossy. Fold half egg white mixture into chocolate mixture until well mixed. Repeat with remaining egg white mixture. Pour into four or six individual dishes or one large one. Chill until firm. Serve decorated with whipped cream and chocolate.

CHOCOLATE LIQUEUR MOUSSE: Add 1 tablespoon brandy, chocolate or coffee liqueur to melted chocolate.

ICE-CREAM

4 eggs, separated
¼ cup caster sugar

¼ cup caster sugar
1 teaspoon vanilla essence
300 ml cream

Beat egg whites until stiff peaks form. Gradually add first measure of sugar, 1 table-spoon at a time, beating until sugar dissolves before adding the next tablespoon. In a separate bowl beat egg yolks and second measure of sugar until thick and pale. Add vanilla. Gently fold yolk mixture into egg white mixture. In another bowl beat cream until thick then fold into egg mixture. Pour mixture into a shallow container suitable for freezing. Freeze for 3–4 hours or until firm.

Variations

Any of the following can be added after the cream:
1 cup chocolate chips

1 cup chopped nuts
1 cup puréed berry fruit, e.g. strawberries, raspberries

ICE-CREAM PUDDING

50 g butter
¼ cup sugar
¼ cup Edmonds standard grade flour

1 egg
2 cups milk
½ teaspoon vanilla essence

Cream butter and sugar until pale. Stir in flour. Lightly beat egg with a fork. Add to creamed mixture. In a saucepan, mix creamed mixture and milk together. Cook over a low heat until mixture boils and thickens, stirring constantly. Remove from heat. Add vanilla. Pour into serving dish. Chill until set.

MELROSE CREAM

2 tablespoons Edmonds
custard powder
1 tablespoon sugar

2 cups milk
85 g packet jelly crystals

In a saucepan mix custard powder, sugar and ¼ cup of the milk to a smooth paste. Add remaining milk and cook, stirring constantly until mixture boils and thickens. Remove from heat. Cover and set aside. Make jelly according to packet directions. Allow to cool. Combine jelly and custard. Pour into a wet mould. Chill until set. Unmould onto a serving plate.

MERINGUES

2 egg whites
½ cup caster sugar

whipped cream

Preheat oven to 120°C. Using an electric mixer, beat egg whites until stiff but not dry. Add half the sugar and beat well. Repeat with remaining sugar. Pipe or spoon small amounts of meringue onto a greased oven tray. Bake at 120°C for 1 to 1½ hours or until the meringues are dry but not brown. Cool. Store unfilled meringues in an airtight container. To serve sandwich together with whipped cream or serve as an accompaniment to fresh fruit salad and whipped cream.

ORIENTAL SUNDAE

2 packets jelly crystals (any flavour)
2 cups boiling water
1 sponge cake

variety of fruit: peaches, apricots, oranges, pineapple (canned), passionfruit, etc.

Cut sponge into small squares and put layer of sponge and layer of fruit into bowl. Dissolve jelly crystals in the boiling water and when cool pour over mixture. Leave until set and serve with cream or Edmonds Custard.

PAVLOVA

4 egg whites
1½ cups caster sugar
1 teaspoon white vinegar
1 teaspoon vanilla essence

1 tablespoon Edmonds Fielder's cornflour
whipped cream
fresh berries and mint leaves, to garnish

Preheat oven to 180°C. Using an electric mixer, beat egg whites and caster sugar for 10 to 15 minutes or until thick and glossy. Mix vinegar, essence and cornflour together. Add to meringue. Beat on high speed for a further 5 minutes. Line an oven tray with baking paper. Draw a 22 cm circle on the baking paper. Spread the pavlova to within 2 cm of the edge of the circle, keeping the shape as round and even as possible. Smooth top surface. Place pavlova in preheated oven then turn oven temperature down to 100°C. Bake pavlova for 1 hour. Turn off oven. Open oven door slightly and leave pavlova in oven until cold. Carefully lift pavlova onto a serving plate. Decorate with whipped cream, fresh berries and mint leaves.

On every birthday or special event I use the Edmonds cookbook to make a Pavlova. After years of using this recipe, I have now been dubbed the 'pavlova queen'. Thank you Edmonds.
                                                                                    KAREN

PINEAPPLE SNOW

SERVES 6

440 g can pineapple pieces
85 g packet pineapple jelly crystals

1½ cups boiling water
2 egg whites

Drain pineapple, reserving all the juice. Place pineapple into a serving dish. Place jelly crystals into bowl. Add boiling water. Stir to dissolve sugar. Add reserved pineapple juice. Chill until consistency of raw egg white. Beat egg whites until stiff. Combine egg whites and jelly. Beat together until thick. Pour over pineapple in serving dish. Chill until set.

SPANISH CREAM

SERVES 6

1 tablespoon gelatine
2 tablespoons water
2 eggs, separated

¼ cup sugar
2 cups milk
1 teaspoon vanilla essence

Combine gelatine and water. Leave to swell for 10 minutes. In a bowl beat egg yolks and sugar until pale. Pour milk and egg mixture into the top of a double boiler. Cook over a low heat, stirring constantly until mixture thickens to coat the back of a wooden spoon. Remove from heat. Add vanilla. Dissolve gelatine over hot water. Stir gelatine into custard mixture. Chill until consistency of raw egg white. Beat egg whites until stiff. Fold into custard mixture. Pour into a wet mould. Chill until firm. Unmould onto a serving plate.

TRIFLE

SERVES 6

4 tablespoons Edmonds custard powder
3 tablespoons sugar
2 cups milk
225 g Ernest Adams unfilled sponge
¼ cup raspberry or apricot jam
¼ cup sherry

410 g can fruit salad
¾ cup cream
2 teaspoons icing sugar
¼ cup toasted slivered almonds to
   decorate

To make the custard, mix custard powder, sugar and ¼ cup of the milk to a smooth paste in a saucepan. Add remaining milk and stir over a low heat until mixture comes to the boil. Simmer for 2 to 3 minutes or until custard thickens, stirring constantly. Remove from heat, cover and leave until cold. Cut sponges in half horizontally. Spread cut surfaces with jam. Sandwich halves together. Cut into cubes then arrange in 6 individual serving dishes or 1 large serving bowl. Spoon sherry over sponge. Spoon fruit salad and juice evenly over sponge. Spoon custard over fruit salad. Chill until set. Beat cream and icing sugar until thick. Decorate trifles with cream and almonds.

TO SPEED UP THE COOLING OF THE CUSTARD, TRANSFER MIXTURE FROM THE SAUCEPAN TO A HEATPROOF BOWL. STAND IN A BOWL OF ICED WATER.

PUDDINGS

My favourite Edmonds recipe is the Carrot Plum Pudding. This recipe disappeared long ago from the cookbook and caused me recently to pay a high price for a 1968 edition which contains it. In my early flatting days I used to make one of these and use half for pudding and the other half sliced and buttered for cut lunches — like a fruit loaf. This was in the 1960s, before carrot cake became 'trendy'!

ROY SINGLETON, WELLINGTON

We have enjoyed so many recipes from our Edmonds cookbooks over the years. It has always been a staple in our homes both here and overseas. Our all-time favourite would have to be Chocolate Self-Saucing Pudding. Yum! Our whole family has fond memories of this pud on cold stormy nights and even cold for breakfast. This is one of the first recipes that my kids learnt to make and now when they all come home it is one of their first requests.

JONELLE MATTHEWS, ST ALBANS, CHRISTCHURCH

I remember back in the late forties being very miffed when the Lemon Cheese Pudding was served at a dinner when a visitor increased our table setting from three to four so I was denied a second helping of my favourite dish. It was often served with cream begged for at the back door of the local dairy when rationing limited cream supplies.

JOHN BEAN, PAPATOETOE, AUCKLAND

My favourite recipe is Pancakes. As a man who doesn't cook very often I did manage to make Pancakes with my trusty Edmonds recipe book. It was a real favourite when the children were small as I used to toss them in the air to turn them. It was cause for much laughter from the children when they missed the pan on the way down and finished up on the floor or on the stove top!

DAVID LEES, HAMILTON

I was one of four children and our mother would usually make Rice Pudding when we had our weekly roast. There was no pudding until we had eaten all our dinner and one of the four of us would get to serve the Rice Pudding. Whoever served it into the plates was the last to choose their serve. Consequently, they were all equal, just about to the last grain of rice! I used to make it for my children and it is still a special treat for my husband and myself.

SUE PARKER, ALBANY, AUCKLAND

One of our all-time favourites is the Sago Plum Pudding. I remember my mum making it when we were small as our Christmas plum pudding. It was so popular she'd make it other times too. Then I started making it when my family was growing up. Then my children grew up and went to live in Perth (all three of them). First my daughter requested a copy of the Edmonds Cookery Book (couldn't find a decent Oz recipe book, she said). But brother borrowed it and wouldn't give it back. So had to send her another. Guess who makes the Sago Plum Puddings now. Yes, into the third generation. My mum and I now provide homestay for overseas students, and they just love the Sago Plum Pudding too. I think this recipe is on its way around the world.

THERESA ADAMS, GLENFIELD, AUCKLAND

BAKED LEMON CHEESECAKE

SERVES 8 TO 10

BASE
1 cup plain biscuit crumbs
50 g butter, melted

FILLING
500 g cream cheese, softened
250 g sour cream

1 cup caster sugar
2 tablespoons Edmonds standard
    grade flour
1 tablespoon finely grated lemon zest
¼ cup lemon juice
3 eggs, lightly beaten

Preheat oven to 150°C. To make the base, combine biscuit crumbs and butter. Mix well. Press evenly over the base of a 20 cm diameter springform tin. Refrigerate while preparing the filling. Place cream cheese, sour cream, sugar, flour, lemon zest and juice in a food processor. Blend till smooth. With the motor running on slow speed, gradually add eggs, processing until well blended. Pour filling into tin. Bake at 150°C for 1 hour 50 minutes or until firm. Cool in tin. Cover and refrigerate for at least 6 hours before serving.

BREAD AND BUTTER PUDDING

SERVES 6

4 × 2 cm thick slices stale spiced fruit bread
4 eggs
1 cup full cream milk
½ cup cream

1 teaspoon grated lemon zest
icing sugar
lemon zest, to garnish

Preheat oven to 180°C. Thoroughly grease a baking dish or 6 individual breakfast cups. Cut fruit bread into quarters and arrange over the base of the dish or cups. Beat eggs, milk, cream and lemon zest together until combined. Pour through a sieve over bread. Place baking dish or cups in a large baking dish. Pour in hot water to come halfway to three-quarters of the way up the dish or cups. Bake in the bain marie for 30 to 35 minutes or until set. Serve dusted with icing sugar and garnished with lemon zest.

CARROT PLUM PUDDING

SERVES 6

1 cup Edmonds standard grade flour
½ cup sugar
1 teaspoon cinnamon
1 teaspoon mixed spice
pinch of salt
1 packed cup of grated carrot

1 cup mixed dried fruit (eg currants, raisins,
    sultanas)
1 teaspoon baking soda
¾ cup warm milk
1 tablespoon butter, melted

Combine flour, sugar, spices and salt in a mixing bowl. Stir in carrot and fruit. Dissolve baking soda in the warm milk. Stir in butter. Stir into dry ingredients. Transfer to a greased 4–5 cup capacity steam pudding basin or heatproof bowl. Cover with greased baking paper or foil. Secure with string. Steam in a covered saucepan of simmering water (water should come halfway to three-quarters of the way up sides of pudding basin) for 2½ hours or until pudding feels firm to touch.

CHOCOLATE SELF-SAUCING PUDDING

100 g butter, softened
¾ cup sugar
1 egg
1 teaspoon vanilla essence
1¼ cups Edmonds standard grade flour
2 teaspoons Edmonds baking powder

1 tablespoon cocoa
½ cup brown sugar
1 tablespoon Edmonds Fielder's cornflour
2 tablespoons cocoa
2 cups boiling water

Preheat oven to 180°C. Beat butter, sugar, egg and essence together. Sift flour, baking powder and first measure of cocoa together. Fold into beaten mixture. Spoon mixture into a greased ovenproof dish. Combine brown sugar, cornflour and second measure of cocoa. Sprinkle over batter. Carefully pour boiling water over the back of a spoon onto the pudding. Bake for 35 minutes or until pudding springs back when lightly touched.

CHRISTMAS PUDDING 1

SERVES 6

1 cup sultanas
1 cup raisins
1 cup currants
70 g packet blanched almonds, chopped
150 g packet mixed peel
1 cup shredded suet
1 cup Edmonds standard grade flour
1½ teaspoons Edmonds baking powder
1 teaspoon mixed spice

1 teaspoon cinnamon
¼ teaspoon ground nutmeg
¼ teaspoon salt
1½ cups soft breadcrumbs
1 cup brown sugar
2 eggs
2 teaspoons grated lemon zest
½ cup milk
1 tablespoon brandy

Put sultanas, raisins, currants, almonds and mixed peel into a large bowl. Add suet, mixing to combine. Sift flour, baking powder, mixed spice, cinnamon, nutmeg and salt into fruit mixture. Stir well. Add breadcrumbs and mix through. In a separate bowl, beat brown sugar, eggs, lemon zest and milk together. Add to fruit mixture, mixing thoroughly to combine. Stir in brandy. Spoon mixture into a well-greased 6-cup-capacity pudding basin. Cover with pleated baking paper or foil. Secure with string, leaving a loop to lift out pudding when cooked. Place a trivet or old saucer in the bottom of a large saucepan half-filled with boiling water. Carefully lower pudding into saucepan making sure the water comes two-thirds of the way up the sides of basin. Cover and cook for 5 hours, making sure water is constantly bubbling. Check water level from time to time. Remove from saucepan. Leave until cold. Wrap well and store in refrigerator until ready to use. Steam for a further 2 hours before serving.

CHRISTMAS PUDDING 2

175 g sultanas
175 g raisins
175 g currants
75 g blanched almonds
175 g mixed peel
grated rind of ½ lemon
175 g breadcrumbs
250 g shredded suet
175 g brown sugar

125 g Edmonds standard grade flour
1½ teaspoons Edmonds baking powder
1 teaspoon mixed spice
1 teaspoon cinnamon
½ teaspoon nutmeg
½ teaspoon salt
2 eggs
150 ml milk, about
1 tablespoon brandy

Combine dried fruit, lemon rind, suet, breadcrumbs and brown sugar. Combine flour, baking powder, spices and salt. Stir through fruit. Fold in beaten eggs, milk and brandy. Put into a well-greased 6 cup capacity pudding basin. Cover with paper or foil and secure with string. Place a trivet or old saucer in the bottom of a large saucepan half filled with boiling water. Carefully lower pudding into saucepan making sure water comes two-thirds of the way up the sides of the basin. Cover and steam for 5 hours, making sure water is constantly boiling. Check water level from time to time. Remove from saucepan. Leave until cold. Wrap well and refrigerate until ready to use. Steam 2 hours more on Christmas Day.

GOOSEBERRY SHORTCAKE

225 g Edmonds standard grade flour
1 teaspoon Edmonds baking powder
125 g butter
1 egg

2 teaspoons sugar
gooseberries
sugar to sprinkle
icing sugar to dust

Preheat oven to 200°C. Sift flour and baking powder. Rub in butter until mixture resembles coarse breadcrumbs. Beat egg and sugar until thick, mix into flour to make a light paste. Cut in half. Roll out one piece 2 cm thick, and place on a cold greased oven tray, cover with gooseberries (which have been topped and tailed), sprinkle over a little sugar. Place other piece on top, close edges, and bake for 20 to 30 minutes at 200°C. Sprinkle with icing sugar and cut while hot.

HARLEQUIN PUDDING

50 g butter, softened
5 tablespoons sugar
1 egg
¾ cup Edmonds standard grade flour
2 tablespoons Edmonds custard powder

1 teaspoon Edmonds baking powder
¼ cup milk
1 cup raisins
1 tablespoon cocoa

Cream butter and sugar together until light and fluffy. Add egg, beating well. Sift flour, custard powder and baking powder together. Fold into creamed mixture. Stir in milk. Place raisins in a well-greased 2-cup-capacity pudding basin. Spoon half the mixture on top. Stir cocoa into remaining mixture. Spoon this on top of plain mixture. Cover with pleated baking paper or foil. Secure with string. Steam in a covered saucepan of simmering water (water should come halfway to three-quarters of the way up sides of the pudding basin) for 30 minutes or until mixture feels firm when touched. Unmould onto a serving plate.

LEMON CHEESE PUDDING

1 tablespoon butter
½ cup sugar
2 tablespoons Edmonds standard
   grade flour

⅛ teaspoon salt
rind and juice of 1 lemon
1 cup milk
2 eggs, separated

Preheat over to 160°C. Cream butter and sugar. Add flour, salt, lemon rind and juice, then milk and egg yolks. In a separate bowl, beat egg whites until stiff. Fold into pudding mixture. Transfer to a greased ovenproof dish. Stand dish in a pan of hot water. Bake at 160°C for 40 minutes. Do not overcook.

MYSTERIOUS PUDDING

1 tablespoon jam or marmalade
50 g butter, softened
¼ cup sugar
1 tablespoon grated lemon or orange rind

2 eggs, separated
1 cup Edmonds standard grade flour
1 teaspoon Edmonds baking powder
½ cup milk

Grease a 3–4 cup capacity steam pudding basin or heatproof bowl. Place jam in the bottom. Cream butter and sugar. Add rind and egg yolks and beat well. In a separate bowl, beat egg whites until stiff. Fold into pudding mixture. Sift flour and baking powder. Fold into mixture alternately with milk. Transfer to prepared basin. Cover with baking paper or foil. Secure with string. Steam in a covered saucepan of simmering water (water should come halfway to three-quarters of the way up sides of the pudding basin) for 1¼ hours or until pudding feels firm to touch. Serve with jam or Edmonds custard.

TO MAKE A CUSTARD.

From a pint of new milk take enough to mix smooth one large dessertspoonful of Edmonds' Custard Powder, sweeten the remainder of the milk to taste (say, a heaped dessertspoonful sugar), and when the milk is boiling, pour the mixed custard into it, stir and pour immediately into jug. When cold, place in glasses (grate nutmeg on if desired).

This Custard Recipe applies to Rice, Sago, Tapioca, and Bread and Butter Puddings, also as creamings for all Stewed Fruits.

FROM EDMONDS CHUTNEYS, PESTOS, JAMS & OTHER PRESERVES (2000).

OVERNIGHT PUDDING

2 teaspoons Edmonds baking soda,
    dissolved in 1 cup cold water
1 teaspoon butter, dissolved in 1 cup
    hot water
1 cup currants

1 cup sultanas
50 g mixed peel
2 cups Edmonds standard grade flour
1 cup sugar
1 teaspoon mixed spice

Mix the 2 cups of liquid together, and pour over prepared fruit and dry ingredients.
Stir well, and stand overnight. In the morning, mix well again. Tie in a cloth and boil
for 3 hours. This pudding may be put in a greased basin and steamed if preferred.

PANCAKES   SERVES 4

1 cup Edmonds standard grade flour
⅛ teaspoon salt

1 egg
about 1 cup milk

Sift flour and salt into a bowl. Add egg, mixing to combine. Gradually beat in sufficient
milk to mix to a smooth batter. Chill for 1 hour. Stir. The batter will thicken on
standing. Heat a greased pancake pan or small frying pan. Pour in just enough batter
to cover base of pan. Cook until golden on underside. Release with knife around edges.
Flip or turn and cook other side. Stack pancakes as you cook.

POORMAN'S CHRISTMAS PUDDING   SERVES 6 TO 8

1 cup Edmonds standard grade flour
1 teaspoon Edmonds baking powder
1 teaspoon mixed spice
1 cup raisins
1 cup currants
125 g chopped blanched almonds

1 cup sugar
1 cup fresh breadcrumbs
1 cup shredded suet
pinch of salt
2 eggs, beaten
milk to mix (about ¾ cup)

Grease a 6 cup capacity steam pudding basin or heatproof bowl. Sift flour, baking
powder and mixed spice. Stir in raisins, currants, almonds, sugar, breadcrumbs, suet
and salt. Stir in eggs and sufficient milk to mix to a spoonable consistency. Transfer
to prepared basin. Cover with baking paper or foil. Secure with string. Steam in a
covered saucepan of simmering water (water should come halfway to three-quarters
of the way up sides of the pudding basin) for 3 hours or until pudding feels firm to
touch. Serve with Edmonds custard.

QUEEN OF PUDDINGS

2 eggs, separated
2 cups milk
2 tablespoons sugar

1 cup soft breadcrumbs or cakecrumbs
2 tablespoons raspberry jam
¼ cup sugar

Preheat oven to 160°C. Beat egg yolks, milk and sugar together. Place breadcrumbs in bottom of a greased ovenproof dish. Pour in egg yolk mixture. Bake at 160°C for 30 minutes or until set. Remove from oven and allow to cool. Spread with jam. Increase oven temperature to 200°C. Beat egg whites until stiff but not dry. Gradually beat in sugar, 1 tablespoon at a time, until sugar has dissolved. Spoon or pipe meringue on top of pudding. Return to oven and bake at 200°C for 10 minutes or until golden.

VARIATION
Add 1 teaspoon grated lemon rind and 1 teaspoon vanilla essence.

RICE PUDDING

SERVES 4

5 tablespoons short grain rice
2 tablespoons sugar
3 cups milk

2 to 3 drops vanilla essence
1 teaspoon butter
¼ teaspoon ground nutmeg

Preheat oven to 150°C. Place rice and sugar in bottom of an ovenproof dish. Add milk and essence. Mix well. Add butter. Sprinkle nutmeg over surface. Bake for 2 hours, stirring 2 to 3 times in first hour. This pudding should be creamy when cooked.

SAGO PUDDING
Omit rice and replace with 3 tablespoons sago.

SAGO PLUM PUDDING

4 tablespoons sago
1 cup milk
75 g breadcrumbs
1 tablespoon melted butter

½ teaspoon Edmonds baking soda
125 g sultanas
125 g currants
75 g sugar

Soak sago in milk and leave overnight. Next day, add breadcrumbs, melted butter, baking soda, prepared fruit and sugar. Put into a greased basin, cover with baking paper and steam for 3 hours. Serve with Edmonds Custard.

SNOW PUDDING

1 tablespoon gelatine
½ cup cold water
½ cup boiling water

2 egg whites
2 tablespoons sugar
vanilla essence

Soften gelatine in cold water; add boiling water. Beat egg whites until stiff; add sugar, vanilla and dissolved gelatine. Beat well and pour into greased cake tin lined with baking paper. When set, turn out and decorate with whipped cream and fruit.

SPONGE ROLL

3 eggs
pinch of salt
½ cup caster sugar
½ teaspoon vanilla essence
5 tablespoons Edmonds standard
   grade flour

1 teaspoon Edmonds baking powder
25 g butter, melted
caster or icing sugar

jam or honey to spread
whipped cream

Preheat oven to 200°C. Grease a 20 × 30 cm sponge-roll tin. Using an electric mixer, beat eggs and salt for 2 minutes. Add sugar and essence and beat until thick and pale. Sift flour and baking powder together. Fold lightly into egg mixture. Fold in butter. Pour into prepared tin. Bake for 8 to 10 minutes or until golden and cake springs back when lightly touched. Turn out onto a cloth or baking paper sprinkled with caster or icing sugar. Trim edges. Roll into a log, including the cloth or paper in the roll and working from the short side. Set aside until cold. Carefully unroll log. Spread with jam or honey, then whipped cream. Again roll from the short side but do not include the cloth or paper this time. To serve, cut into slices using a sharp knife.

STEAMED RAINBOW PUDDING   SERVES 4

75 g butter, softened
75 g sugar
1 teaspoon vanilla essence
175 g Edmonds standard grade flour
1 teaspoon Edmonds baking powder

pinch of salt
2 eggs, beaten
¼ cup milk
1 teaspoon cocoa
few drops red food colouring

Grease a 3–4 cup capacity steam pudding basin or heatproof bowl. Cream butter, sugar and essence. Sift flour, baking powder and salt. Combine eggs and milk. Fold into creamed mixture alternately with flour. Divide mixture into three equal portions. Leave one as is, stir cocoa into another and finally, a few drops of food colouring into the last mixture. Drop spoonfuls of each of the mixture randomly into prepared basin, so the pudding will have a marbled effect when cut. Cover with baking paper or foil. Secure with string. Steam in a covered saucepan of simmering water (water should come halfway to three-quarters of the way up sides of the pudding basin) for 1½–2 hours or until pudding feels firm to touch. Serve with Edmonds custard.

STEAMED SPONGE PUDDING

100 g butter, softened
½ cup sugar
2 eggs
¼ cup apricot jam
2 cups Edmonds standard grade flour

2 teaspoons Edmonds baking powder
¼ teaspoon salt
1 teaspoon Edmonds baking soda
1 cup milk

Cream butter and sugar until light and fluffy. Add eggs, beating well. Stir in jam. Sift flour, baking powder and salt into creamed mixture, then fold in. Dissolve baking soda in milk and add to mixture. Spoon mixture into a greased 4-cup-capacity pudding basin. Cover with baking paper or foil. Secure with string. Steam in a covered saucepan of simmering water (water should come halfway to three-quarters of the way up sides of the pudding basin) for 60 minutes or until pudding feels firm to touch.

GOLDEN SYRUP STEAMED SPONGE PUDDING
Place 1 tablespoon golden syrup at the bottom of pudding basin.

APPLE STEAMED SPONGE PUDDING
Mix ½ cup stewed apple into mixture.

FIG OR PRUNE STEAMED SPONGE PUDDING
Mix ½ cup chopped figs or prunes into mixture.

THREE-QUARTER HOUR PUDDING

1 cup Edmonds standard grade flour
1 teaspoon Edmonds baking powder
¼ teaspoon salt
1 tablespoon sugar
1 tablespoon butter
milk to mix (about ⅔ cup)

SYRUP
2 tablespoons sugar
1 tablespoon golden syrup or honey
1 cup boiling water

Grease a 3–4 cup capacity steam pudding basin or heatproof bowl. Sift flour, baking powder and salt. Stir in sugar. Rub in butter. Add sufficient milk to mix to a soft dough. Transfer to prepared basin. Pour over syrup. To make syrup, dissolve sugar and golden syrup in the water. Do not cover the basin. Stand in a saucepan of boiling water (water to come halfway up sides of basin). Put lid on saucepan and steam for 45 minutes or until pudding is firm to touch.

My favourite is the Three-Quarter Hour Pudding — with cocoa and raisins added. When we were growing up on the farm, from the age of eleven, we had to take turns making dessert each night. I loved making this steamed pudding.

DENE BUSBY, ST HELIERS, AUCKLAND

SWEETS

My favourite recipe is Chocolate Fudge in the sweets section. I first learned to make this when I was a teenager, and that was many decades ago! I am known by my family as the expert fudge maker. It never fails to satisfy a sweet tooth. I've even been known to whip it up at parties when things get dull. I've made it in several different countries as well, and regardless of the variation in local ingredients, it's always a winner. (How much variation could there really be in butter, sugar, and cocoa?!) Even though the recipe is burned into my brain, I still turn to the cocoa-speckled page when it comes time to whip up a batch.

ANNE KERSLAKE HENDRICKS, KELBURN, WELLINGTON

I made a batch of Chocolate Fudge and a batch of Russian Fudge to take to my family last year for Christmas lunch, however my immediate family, boyfriend and myself ended up eating most of it before Christmas Day. I was lucky to scrape ten pieces of each to put aside for Christmas Day! That left only one piece of fudge per person on the day! Whoops!

KIRSTY REYNOLDS, HIGHLAND PARK, AUCKLAND

Almond Toffee is great and easy to make and is especially suitable for our children who have severe food allergies. (Of course we make it without the nuts.)

MIKE & JULIE CARTER, BISHOPDALE, CHRISTCHURCH

CHOCOLATE FUDGE

2 cups sugar
2 tablespoons cocoa
½ cup milk
25 g butter

½ teaspoon vanilla
  essence
½ cup chopped walnuts (optional)

Put sugar and cocoa into a saucepan. Mix to combine. Add milk and butter. Heat gently, stirring constantly until sugar has dissolved and butter has melted. Bring to the boil. Do not stir. Let mixture boil until the soft ball stage. To test for soft ball stage, drop a small amount of mixture off a teaspoon into cold water. When a soft ball forms, the mixture is ready. On a sugar thermometer, the soft ball stage is 116°C. Remove from heat. Add essence and leave to stand for 5 minutes. Stir in walnuts. Beat with a wooden spoon until thick. Pour into a buttered tin. Mark into squares. Cut when cold.

FUDGE APPEARED IN SCOTTISH RECIPES IN THE LATE 17TH CENTURY WHEN SUGAR REFINERIES SPRUNG UP ALONGSIDE THE CLYDE RIVER TO PROCESS SUGAR CANE FROM THE WEST INDIES. FUDGE IS ALSO KNOWN AS 'TABLET'.

CHOCOLATE TRUFFLES

50 g butter
100 g cooking chocolate
1 cup icing sugar, approximately

1 tablespoon rum
1 teaspoon cocoa
desiccated coconut, to roll

Put butter and chocolate into a saucepan. Heat gently, stirring until butter and chocolate have melted. Add ½ cup of the icing sugar. Stir until mixture is thick enough to handle. Stir in rum and cocoa. Add enough of the remaining icing sugar to make a stiff mixture. Measure tablespoonsful of the mixture and shape into balls. Roll in coconut. Chill until firm.

COCONUT ICE

4 cups icing sugar
½ cup milk
2 tablespoons butter

¼ teaspoon salt
1 cup desiccated coconut
few drops of red food colouring (optional)

Put icing sugar, milk, butter and salt into a saucepan. Heat gently, stirring constantly until sugar dissolves. Bring to the boil. Do not stir. Let mixture boil until the soft ball stage. To test for soft ball stage, drop a small amount of mixture off a teaspoon into cold water. When a soft ball forms, the mixture is ready. On a sugar thermometer, the soft ball stage is 116°C. Add coconut. Remove from heat and allow to cool for 10 minutes. Beat until mixture starts to thicken. Pour into a buttered tin. Allow to cool. Cut into squares.

Variation

If desired, divide the mixture in half before beating and add a few drops of red food colouring to one portion. Beat the white portion until it starts to thicken. Spread this mixture on top of pink mixture.

FLORENTINE CARAMELS

2½ cups sugar
2 tablespoons desiccated coconut
1 teaspoon ground ginger
1 tablespoon golden syrup

25 g butter
½ cup milk
1 teaspoon vanilla essence

Put sugar, coconut and ginger into a saucepan. Mix to combine. Add golden syrup, butter and milk. Heat gently, stirring constantly until sugar dissolves. Bring to the boil. Do not stir. Boil mixture until the soft ball stage. To test for soft ball stage, drop a small amount of mixture off a teaspoon into cold water. When a soft ball forms, the mixture is ready. On a sugar thermometer, the soft ball stage is 116°C. Remove from the heat. Add vanilla and beat until thick and creamy. Pour into a buttered tin. Mark into squares. Cut when cold.

HOKEY POKEY

5 tablespoons sugar
2 tablespoons golden syrup

1 teaspoon Edmonds baking soda

Put sugar and golden syrup into a saucepan. Heat gently, stirring constantly until sugar dissolves. Increase the heat and bring to the boil. Boil for 2 minutes. Stir occasionally, if necessary, to prevent burning. Remove from heat. Add baking soda. Stir quickly until mixture froths up. Pour into a buttered tin immediately. Leave until cold and hard. Break into pieces.

MARSHMALLOWS

2 tablespoons gelatine
½ cup water
2 cups sugar

1 cup water
1 teaspoon vanilla or peppermint essence
desiccated coconut or icing sugar

Combine gelatine and first measure of water. Leave to swell for 10 minutes. Place sugar and second measure of water in a large saucepan. Heat gently, stirring constantly until sugar dissolves. Dissolve gelatine over hot water. Pour gelatine into sugar mixture and bring to the boil. Boil steadily for 15 minutes. Allow to cool until lukewarm. Beat well until very thick and white. Add vanilla or peppermint essence. Line a large tin with baking paper. Wet baking paper and pour mixture into the tin. Chill until set. Turn out of tin. Cut into squares and roll in coconut or icing sugar. Keep chilled.

RUSSIAN FUDGE

3 cups sugar
½ cup milk
½ cup sweetened condensed milk

125 g butter
⅛ teaspoon salt
1 tablespoon golden syrup

Put sugar and milk into a saucepan. Heat gently, stirring constantly until sugar dissolves. Add condensed milk, butter, salt and golden syrup. Stir until butter has melted. Bring to the boil and continue boiling to the soft ball stage, stirring occasionally to prevent burning. To test for soft ball stage, drop a small amount of mixture off a teaspoon into cold water. When a soft ball forms, the mixture is ready. On a sugar thermometer, the soft ball stage is 116°C. Remove from heat. Cool slightly. Beat until thick. Pour into a buttered tin. Mark into squares. Cut when cold.

VANILLA ESSENCE OR CHOPPED NUTS MAY BE ADDED TO FUDGE BEFORE BEATING.

SHERRY BALLS

1 egg
1 tablespoon cocoa
1½ tablespoons sherry or brandy
¼ cup sugar
125 g butter, melted

250 g packet wine biscuits
2 tablespoons currants
2 tablespoons chopped walnuts
desiccated coconut or chocolate hail

Beat egg, cocoa, brandy and sugar; add butter when lukewarm. Crush biscuits, mix with currants and walnuts, add liquids and mix well. Form into small balls and roll in coconut or chocolate hail. Chill until set (approx. 2 hours).

TOFFEE

2 cups sugar
1 cup water

1 tablespoon white vinegar
1 tablespoon butter

Put sugar, water, vinegar and butter into a saucepan. Heat gently, stirring constantly until sugar dissolves. Bring to the boil. Do not stir. Let mixture boil until a little tried in cold water snaps. Pour into a buttered tin. Mark into squares. Cut when cool.

ALMOND OR ANY NUT TOFFEE

2 cups brown or white sugar
½ cup milk or cream

2 tablespoons butter
½ cup chopped nuts

Put sugar, milk or cream and butter into a saucepan. Bring to the boil, stirring occasionally, then boil without stirring until a little tried in cold water snaps. Add the blanched nuts and pour into a buttered dish.

TOFFEE APPLES

3 cups sugar
1 tablespoon white vinegar
1 tablespoon butter
½ cup water
½ teaspoon cream of tartar

few drops red food colouring
8 apples, approximately
8 wooden ice-block sticks or wooden
   skewers

Put sugar, vinegar, butter and water into a saucepan. Heat gently, stirring constantly until sugar dissolves. Add cream of tartar and food colouring. Bring to the boil. Do not stir. Let mixture boil until a little tried in cold water snaps. While mixture is boiling, wipe the apples. Push an ice-block stick into each stem end. Remove pan from heat, tilt slightly then dip an apple into the toffee, turning to coat. Place on a sheet of baking paper or non-stick foil. Repeat with remaining apples. Leave until cold and set.

There's a rush for Milk Puddings

When the weather is hot and sultry.

The dish that will then tempt the appetite is the cool, delightful Custard with Milk Pudding or luscious fruit.

Nothing is more delicious than a few stewed peaches, pears or apricots, served with custard made with Edmonds' Custard Powder.

There is no element of uncertainty about the success of the custard —if you use Edmonds' you can take the rest for granted.

Let the children have all the custards they want, and like Oliver Twist, they will be "waiting for more."

EDMONDS CUSTARD POWDER

Nott—4167

JAMS & JELLIES

SETTING TESTS FOR JAM AND MARMALADE

Ripeness of fruit, speed of boiling and size of pan are all factors that determine when, and how well, jam or marmalade will set. To know when a jam or marmalade is ready to set, it needs to be tested. Times given in recipes are only a guide. Test frequently to determine when setting point has been reached. Remove the pan from the heat while testing.

TO TEST JAM AND MARMALADE FOR SETTING POINT

Dip a wooden spoon into the jam or marmalade and allow the mixture to drip. When two drops emerge on the end of the spoon instead of running off the spoon, the mixture will set on cooling. Put a little jam or marmalade on a cold plate. Leave to cool slightly. The mixture will set if the surface wrinkles when touched and a channel formed (when a finger is drawn through) remains open. Most jams and marmalades will set at a temperature of 105°C.

APRICOT JAM
MAKES ABOUT 10 × 350 ML JARS

2.7 kg apricots, halved and stoned
10 to 12 apricot kernels

2 ½ cups water
12 cups sugar

Crack a few apricot stones and remove kernels. Put apricots, kernels and water into a preserving pan. Cook over a low heat until fruit is pulpy. Add sugar. Stir until dissolved. Boil briskly for 30 minutes or until setting point is reached. Leave to stand for 4 to 5 minutes. Skim any scum from top of jam. Ladle into hot, clean, dry jars. This jam will keep for up to 1 year.

BLACKCURRANT JAM
MAKES ABOUT 4 × 350 ML JARS

1 kg blackcurrants
2 cups water

6 cups sugar

Remove stalks from blackcurrants. Put blackcurrants and water into a preserving pan. Boil gently until fruit is soft. Add sugar. Stir until dissolved. Bring to the boil and boil rapidly for 15 minutes or until setting point is reached. Pour into sterilised jars.

DRIED APRICOT JAM

1 kg dried apricots
4 litres water

2.7 kg sugar

Wash the apricots very well. Drain, and cover with 4 litres of cold water and allow to stand for two days. Put into preserving pan. Bring to the boil and add sugar; boil for about 30 minutes. Test. A few blanched and chopped almonds are an improvement.

FRUIT SALAD JAM

1 kg apricots, stoned and peeled
1 kg peaches, stoned and peeled
450 g crushed pineapple

10 bananas, peeled
juice of 2 lemons or passionfruit
2.2 kg sugar

Cook all fruit in a large sauepan until soft. Add sugar and simmer for about 20 minutes. Test for setting point. Ladle into hot sterile jars. Seal. Bananas may be omitted.

PEAR AND GINGER JAM

2.7 kg pears
2.1 kg sugar
rind and flesh of 2 lemons,
    finely minced

225 g preserved ginger, chopped
1 cup warm water

Peel and core pears, cut up coarsely. Place in a preserving pan with sugar, lemons, ginger and warm water. Boil gently for 2–2½ hours or until setting point is reached. Pour into hot sterile jars. Seal when cold.

PLUM JAM

MAKES ABOUT 6 × 350 ML JARS

2 kg plums, halved and stoned
7½ cups water

7 cups sugar

Put plums and water into a preserving pan. Boil until soft and pulpy. Add sugar. Stir until dissolved. Boil briskly for 15 minutes or until setting point is reached. Pour into sterilised jars.

One of my favourite memories is making Plum Jam with Mum on the farm, from collecting the fruit to making the jam and picking out the stones and all the kids sucking the jam off the stones. And I'm sure my mum would agree with me.

LINDA HAMMOND, BULLS

RASPBERRY JAM

3 cups raspberries, fresh or frozen   2 ¾ cups sugar

Put the berries into a preserving pan and cook slowly until their juice runs. Bring to the boil. Add sugar and stir until dissolved. Boil briskly for 3 to 5 minutes. Pour into hot, clean, dry jars. Cover with jam covers. This jam firms up after a few days' storage and will keep for up to 1 year.

BOYSENBERRY JAM
Using the recipe above, replace the raspberries with fresh or frozen boysenberries.

STRAWBERRY JAM

1 kg strawberries, hulled   1½ teaspoons tartaric acid
6 cups sugar

Put strawberries into a preserving pan. Crush lightly with a potato masher or fork. Add sugar and stir thoroughly. Bring to the boil. Boil for 5 minutes. Add tartaric acid and boil rapidly for a further 5 minutes. Pour into hot, clean, dry jars. Cover with jam covers. This jam will keep for up to 1 year.

In these modern times it is often cheaper and easier to buy biscuits and cakes, but I still religiously make jams and marmalade. There is something so summery about preparing fruit for jam. It's such a thrill to admire the glowing colours of the completed product before labelling and storing them for the rest of the year. Then to relive the taste of summer berries through the depths of winter and to have the satisfaction, jar by jar, of knowing that I made it myself makes it a labour worth continuing.

DIANE CHAPMAN, OTAKI

TAMARILLO JAM

1.3 kg tamarillos   2 kg sugar
500 g green apples, peeled and minced   juice of 1 lemon
2 cups water

Scald tamarillos, peel and cut up; put with apples into preserving pan with water. Bring to boil and add sugar. Boil until it sets, about 1 hour. Test. Add lemon juice and put into sterilised jars.

MARMALADE

4 large grapefruit, minced, chopped or
   thinly sliced
2 lemons, minced, chopped or thinly sliced

3.4 litres water
sugar

Place grapefruit and lemons in a non-metallic bowl. Cover with the water and stand overnight. Next day, transfer to a saucepan and bring to the boil. Boil for 45 minutes or until fruit is soft and pulpy. Allow to cool a little. Measure pulp and return to pan. Bring to the boil. For each cup of pulp, add 1 cup sugar. Stir until dissolved. Boil briskly, stirring occasionally, until setting point is reached. Pour into hot, clean, dry jars. This marmalade will keep for up to 1 year.

REFRIGERATED ORANGE, LIME AND GINGER MARMALADE

MAKES 4 CUPS

1 litre freshly squeezed orange juice
finely sliced zest of 2 oranges
juice of 6 limes

2½ cups sugar
½ cup chopped crystallised ginger

Combine orange juice, orange zest and lime juice in a large saucepan. Cover pan and bring to the boil. Simmer for 1 hour. Add sugar. Boil uncovered for 30 minutes. Remove from heat. Add ginger. Cool. Transfer to clean jars or containers. Covered and refrigerated, this marmalade will keep for up to 3 months.

SWEET ORANGE MARMALADE

MAKES ABOUT 5 × 350 ML JARS

1.25 kg sweet oranges
2 lemons

1.5 litres water
sugar

Squeeze the juice from the oranges and lemons. Tie pips in a piece of muslin. Finely shred the skins. In a preserving pan, gently boil juice, skins, pips and water for about 1 hour until the skins are tender. Cool a little. Measure pulp and return to pan. Bring to the boil. For each cup of pulp, add 1 cup sugar. Stir until dissolved. Boil briskly for 20 minutes or until setting point is reached. Remove muslin. Pour into sterilised jars.

APPLE JELLY

apples
water
1 cup sugar

cloves
beetroot

Cut up apples without peeling (include cores, etc.). Cover with water and boil to a pulp. Strain through muslin or jelly bag (do not squeeze), then add 1 cup sugar and 1 or 2 cloves to each cup of juice. Boil till it jellies; try on a plate. A few slices of beetroot added to the apples while boiling will improve the colour, or a few drops of red colouring may be added.

BLACKBERRY AND APPLE JELLY   MAKES ABOUT 3 × 250 ML JARS

1 kg blackberries
750 g apples, sliced, unpeeled and uncored

water
sugar

Put blackberries and apples into a preserving pan. Add water to just cover fruit. Cook until fruit is pulpy. Strain through a jelly bag or fine cloth. Measure juice and return to pan. For each cup of juice, add ¾ cup sugar. Bring to the boil, stirring until sugar is dissolved. Boil briskly. Stir occasionally and test for setting after 10 to 15 minutes. When setting point is reached pour into sterilised jars.

QUINCE CONSERVE

4 large quinces
2.2 kg sugar

3.5 litres water

Wipe quinces and place whole in the water; boil until skins crack and are soft. Lift out and skin then cut up quinces. Put sugar into water and when dissolved add fruit. Boil until bright red.

PICKLES, RELISHES & CHUTNEYS

MUSTARD PICKLE

4 cups cauliflower florets
4 cups pickling onions
4 cups diced green tomatoes
4 cups diced cucumber
1¼ cups salt
2 litres water

1 cup Edmonds standard grade flour
4 teaspoons dry mustard
1½ tablespoons turmeric
½ teaspoon cayenne pepper
1 cup sugar
1 litre malt vinegar

Put the prepared vegetables in a large non-metallic bowl. Dissolve the salt in water and pour it over the vegetables. Leave to stand for 24 hours. Drain thoroughly. Mix together flour, mustard, turmeric, cayenne pepper and sugar. Stir in a little of the measured vinegar to make a smooth paste. Gradually add remaining vinegar. Bring to the boil in a large preserving pan, stirring until mixture thickens. Add vegetables and boil for 5 minutes or until vegetables are heated through. Pack into sterilised jars.

PICKLED ONIONS

1.5 kg pickling onions
½ cup salt
water

3 dry chillies, approximately
6 peppercorns, approximately
malt or white vinegar

Place onions in a non-metallic bowl. Sprinkle with salt. Add cold water to cover onions. Stand for 24 hours. Drain and rinse in cold water. Drain again and pack into jars. To each jar add 1 chilli and 2 peppercorns. Add vinegar to cover onions. Seal with non-metallic lids or corks. Store for 4 to 6 weeks before using.

KIWIFRUIT RELISH

500 g kiwifruit, peeled and
    roughly chopped
1 onion, chopped
3 fresh chillies, seeded and finely chopped

1 tablespoon finely chopped fresh ginger
1 cup brown sugar
1 cup cider vinegar

Combine kiwifruit, onion, chillies, ginger, sugar and vinegar in a saucepan. Cook over medium heat for 50 minutes or until mixture is thick and pulpy, stirring frequently. Pack into hot, clean, dry jars. Seal while hot. Sealed, this relish will keep for up to 1 year. Refrigerate after opening.

TOMATO RELISH

1.5 kg tomatoes, blanched, skinned and
   quartered
4 onions, cut into eighths
2 tablespoons salt
2 cups brown sugar
2¼ cups malt vinegar

1 chilli, seeded and
   finely chopped
1 tablespoon dry mustard
1 tablespoon curry powder
2 tablespoons Edmonds standard
   grade flour
¼ cup malt vinegar

Put tomatoes and onions into a non-metallic bowl. Sprinkle with salt and leave for
12 hours. Drain off liquid formed. Put vegetables, sugar, first measure of vinegar and
chilli into a preserving pan. Boil gently for 1½ hours, stirring frequently. Mix mustard,
curry, flour and second measure of vinegar to a smooth paste. Stir into relish. Boil
for 5 minutes. Pack into sterilised jars. Sealed, this relish will keep for up to 1 year.
Refrigerate after opening.

PLUM SAUCE

2.75 kg plums, halved
7 cups malt vinegar
3 cups brown sugar
8 to 10 cloves garlic, peeled and
   finely chopped
2 teaspoons ground pepper

2 teaspoons ground cloves
2 teaspoons ground ginger
1 teaspoon ground mace
¼ teaspoon cayenne pepper
1 tablespoon salt

Put all the ingredients into a preserving pan. Bring to the boil, stirring frequently. Boil
steadily until mixture is pulpy. Press through a colander or coarse sieve. Return sauce
to pan and boil for 2 to 3 minutes. Pour into hot, clean, dry bottles and seal. Sealed,
this sauce will keep for up to 1 year. Refrigerate after opening.

TOMATO SAUCE

3.5 kg tomatoes, chopped
1 kg apples, peeled and chopped
6 onions, chopped
3 cups sugar
4 cups malt vinegar

2 tablespoons salt
½ to 1 teaspoon cayenne pepper
1 teaspoon black peppercorns
1 teaspoon whole allspice
2 teaspoons whole cloves

Put tomatoes, apples, onions, sugar, vinegar, salt and cayenne pepper into a
preserving pan. Tie peppercorns, allspice and cloves in muslin and add. Boil steadily
for about 2 hours or until completely pulpy. Discard whole spices. Press through a
colander or coarse sieve. Return to pan and boil for 2 minutes. Pour into sterilised
bottles and seal.

CASHMERE CHUTNEY

1 kg green gooseberries or apples
malt vinegar
1 kg brown sugar
500 g raisins
500 g dates

1 clove garlic
½ teaspoon cayenne pepper
125 g fresh ginger, chopped and pounded
50 g salt

Put gooseberries, or cored apples chopped but not peeled in preserving pan. Cover with vinegar. Cook until soft, then add remainder of ingredients. Boil half an hour. Put into bottles, seal tightly, and keep 12 months before using.

PEACH CHUTNEY

MAKES ABOUT 4 × 350 ML JARS

2.25 kg peaches, peeled, stoned and
   chopped
500 g onions, chopped
2 cups raisins
1 cup mixed peel
½ cup crystallised ginger, chopped

2 cups brown sugar
1 tablespoon salt
1 tablespoon curry powder
½ teaspoon cayenne pepper
3½ cups malt vinegar

Put all ingredients into a preserving pan. Stir and bring to the boil. Boil steadily with frequent stirring for 1 hour or until mixture is thick and jam-like. Pack into sterilised jars. Cover with preserve seals. This chutney will keep for up to 1 year. Refrigerate after opening.

TOMATO CHUTNEY

MAKES ABOUT 6 × 350 ML JARS

2.25 kg green or firm tomatoes, chopped
6 onions, chopped
1.25 kg apples, peeled and chopped
2 cups seedless raisins
1 cup crystallised peel
4 cups brown sugar

4 cups malt vinegar
2 tablespoons salt
1 teaspoon black peppercorns
2 teaspoons whole cloves
2 chillies

Put tomatoes, onions, apples, raisins, peel, sugar, vinegar and salt into a preserving pan. Tie peppercorns, cloves and chillies in muslin and add. Bring to the boil, stirring. Boil steadily with frequent stirring for about 2 hours or until mixture is thick and jam-like. Remove spice bag and discard. Pack chutney into sterilised jars. Cover with preserve covers. Sealed, this chutney will keep for up to 1 year. Refrigerate after opening.

INDEX